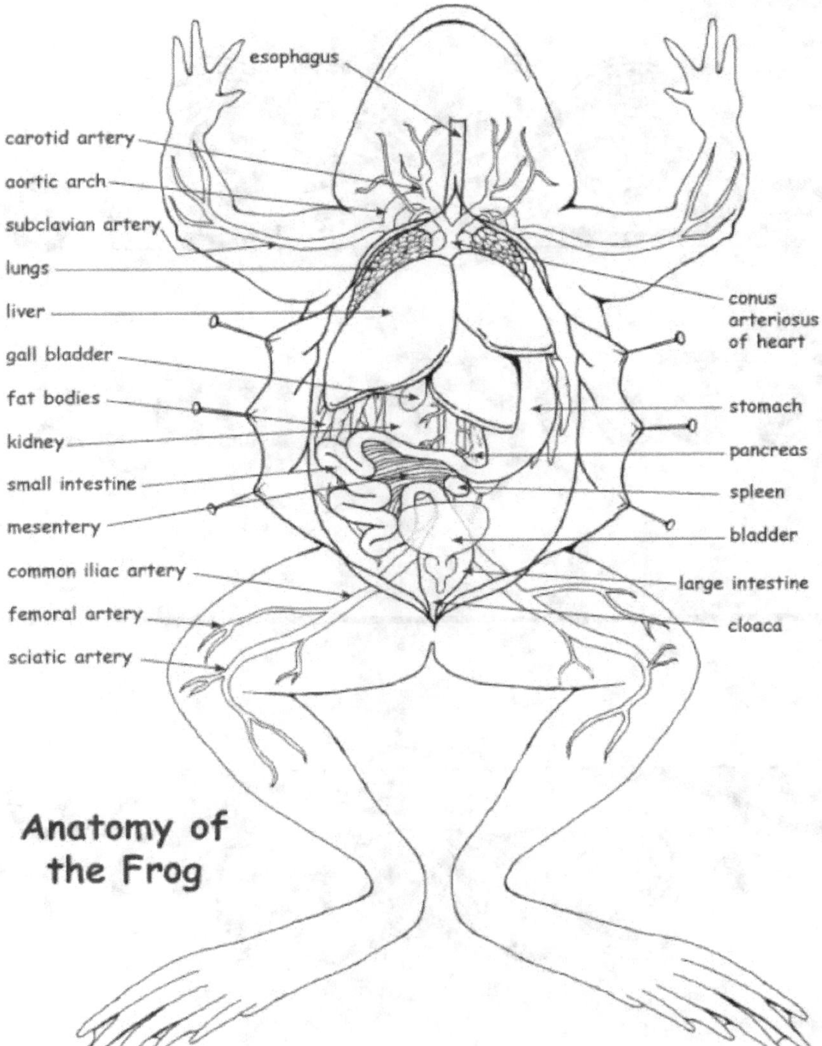


Anatomy of the Frog

# This Book Belongs To

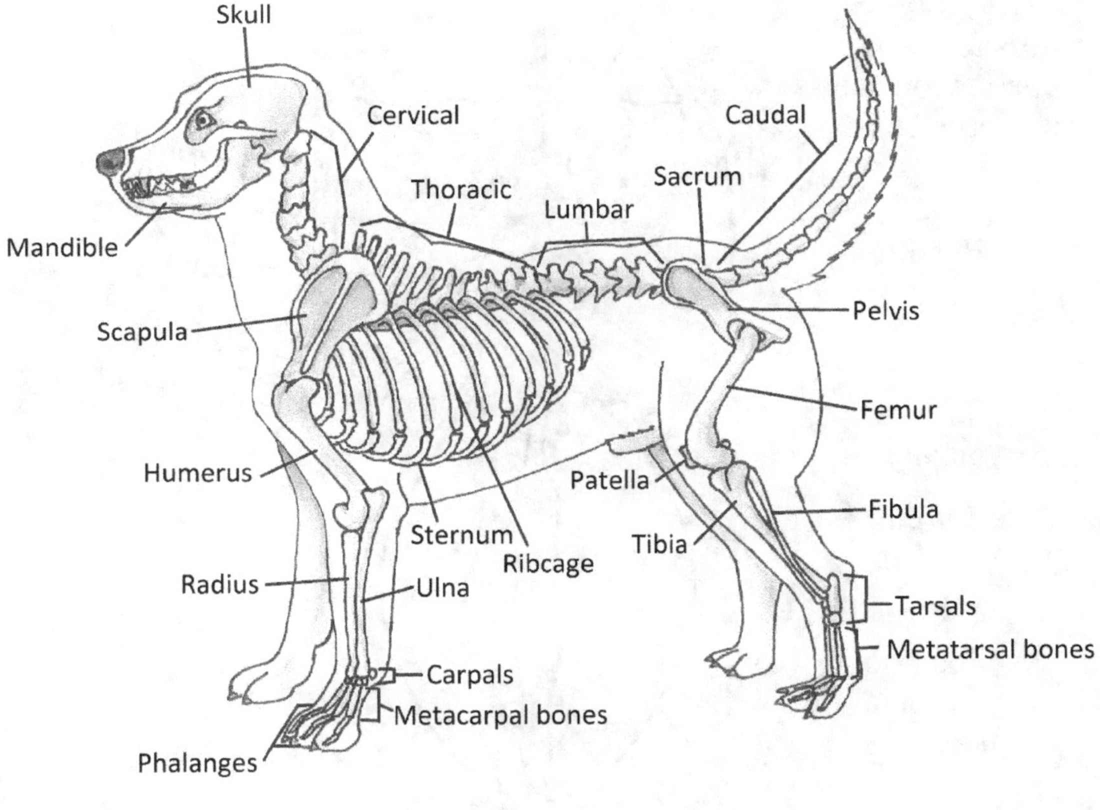

Skull
Cervical
Caudal
Sacrum
Thoracic
Lumbar
Mandible
Pelvis
Scapula
Femur
Humerus
Patella
Fibula
Sternum
Tibia
Ribcage
Radius
Ulna
Tarsals
Metatarsal bones
Carpals
Metacarpal bones
Phalanges

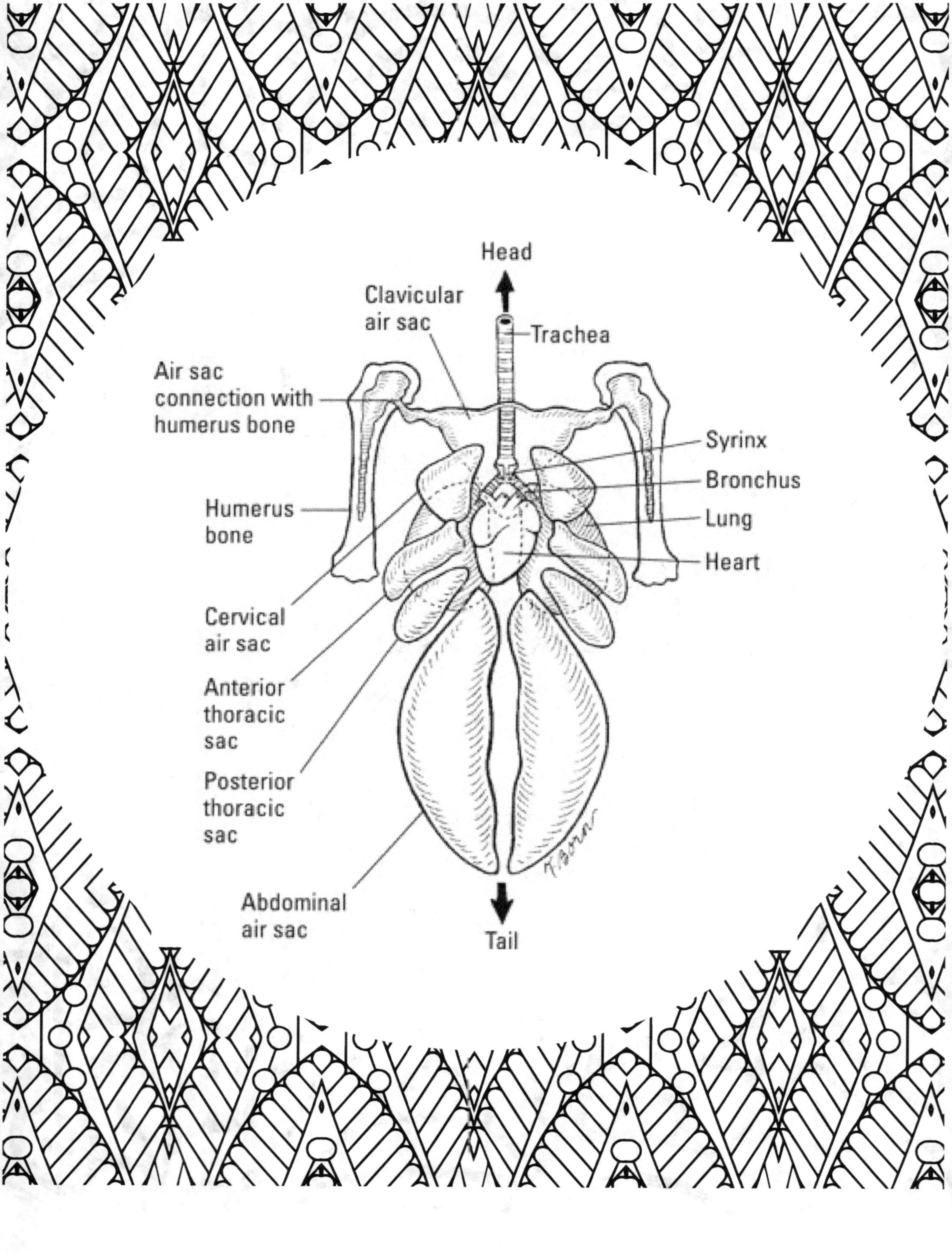
Head
Clavicular air sac
Trachea
Air sac connection with humerus bone
Syrinx
Bronchus
Humerus bone
Lung
Heart
Cervical air sac
Anterior thoracic sac
Posterior thoracic sac
Abdominal air sac
Tail

**Llama Anatomy (Thoracic and Abdominal Organs viewed from the left side)**

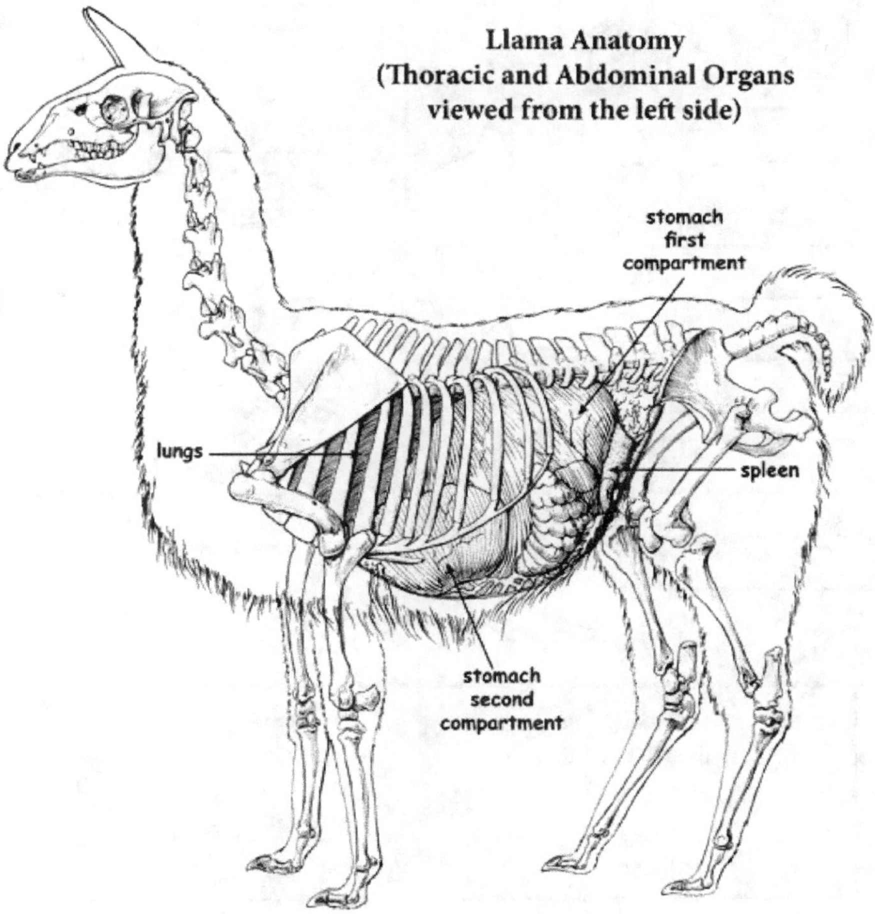

| | |
|---|---|
| cloaca | colon |
| small intestine | gizzard |
| proventriculus | crop |
| esophagus | gallbladder |
| spleen | liver |

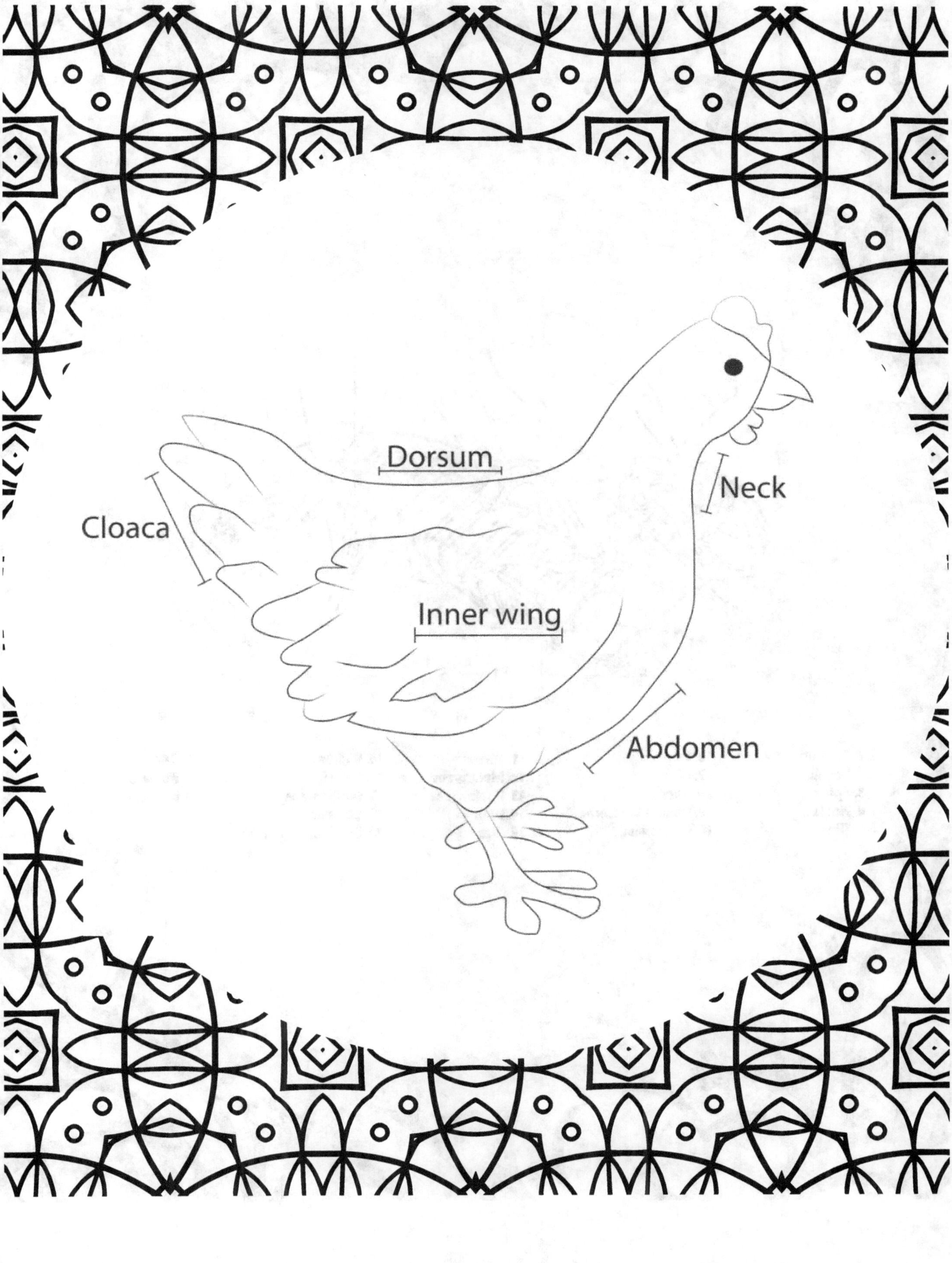
Dorsum
Neck
Cloaca
Inner wing
Abdomen

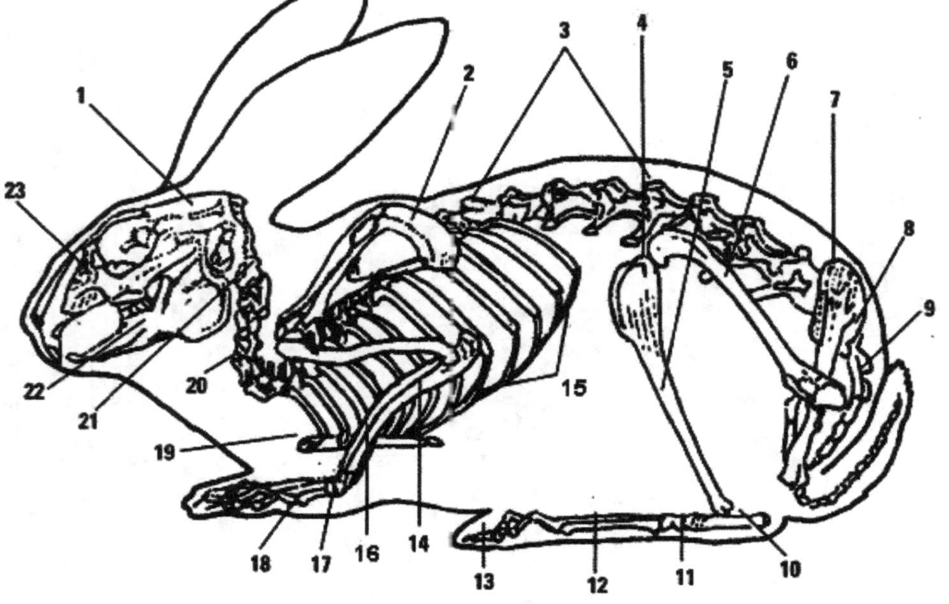


1. Cranium (Skull)
2. Scapula
3. Spine
4. Fibula
5. Tibia
6. Femur
7. Ilium
8. Sacrum
9. Caudal Vertebrae
10. Calcaneus
11. Tarsus
12. Metatarsus
13. Phalanges
14. Ulna
15. Ribs
16. Radius
17. Carpus
18. Metacarpus
19. Sternum
20. Cervical Vertebrae
21. Atlas
22. Mandible
23. Maxilla

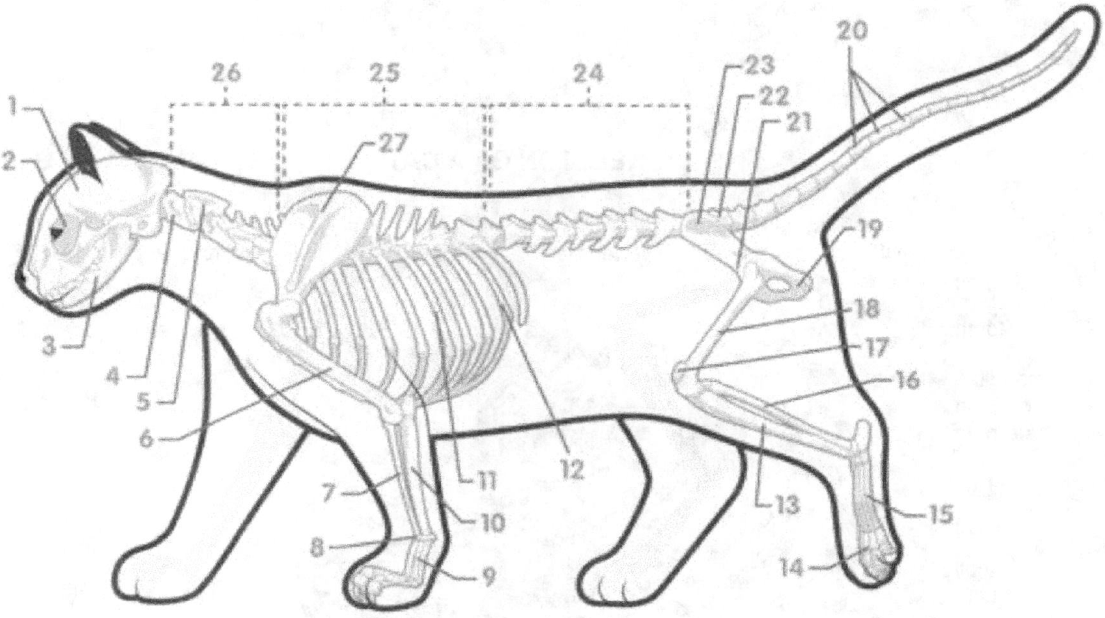


1. Skull
2. Orbit
3. Mandible
4. Atlas
5. Axis
6. Humerus
7. Radius
8. Carpals
9. Metacarpals
10. Ulna
11. Rib
12. Bony part of the rib
13. Tibia
14. Phalanges
15. Metatarsals
16. Fibula
17. Patella
18. Femur
19. Ischium
20. Caudal vertebrae
21. Pubis
22. Sacrum
23. Ilium
24. Lumber vertebrae
25. Thoracic vertebrae
26. Cervical vertebrae
27. Scapula

## SKELETON OF A CAT

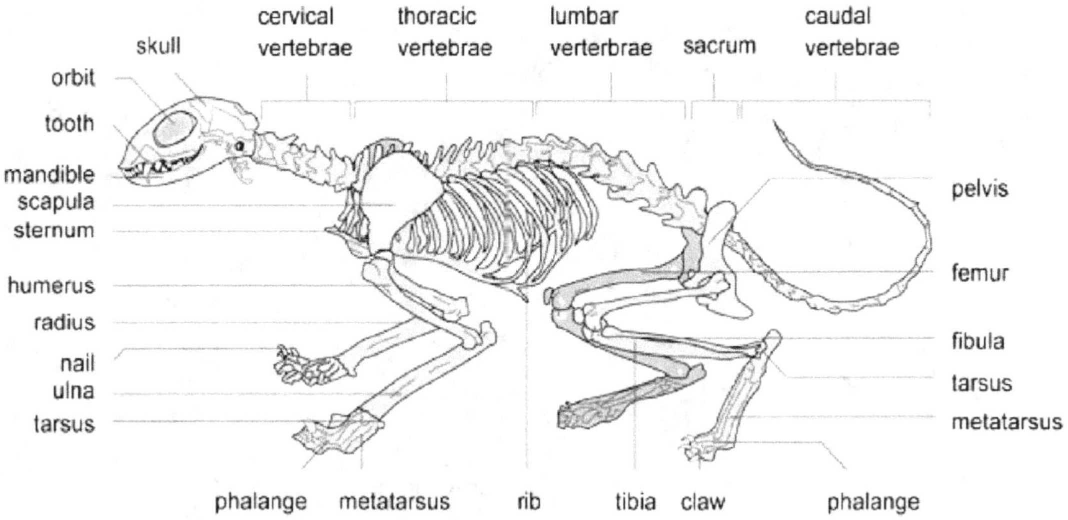

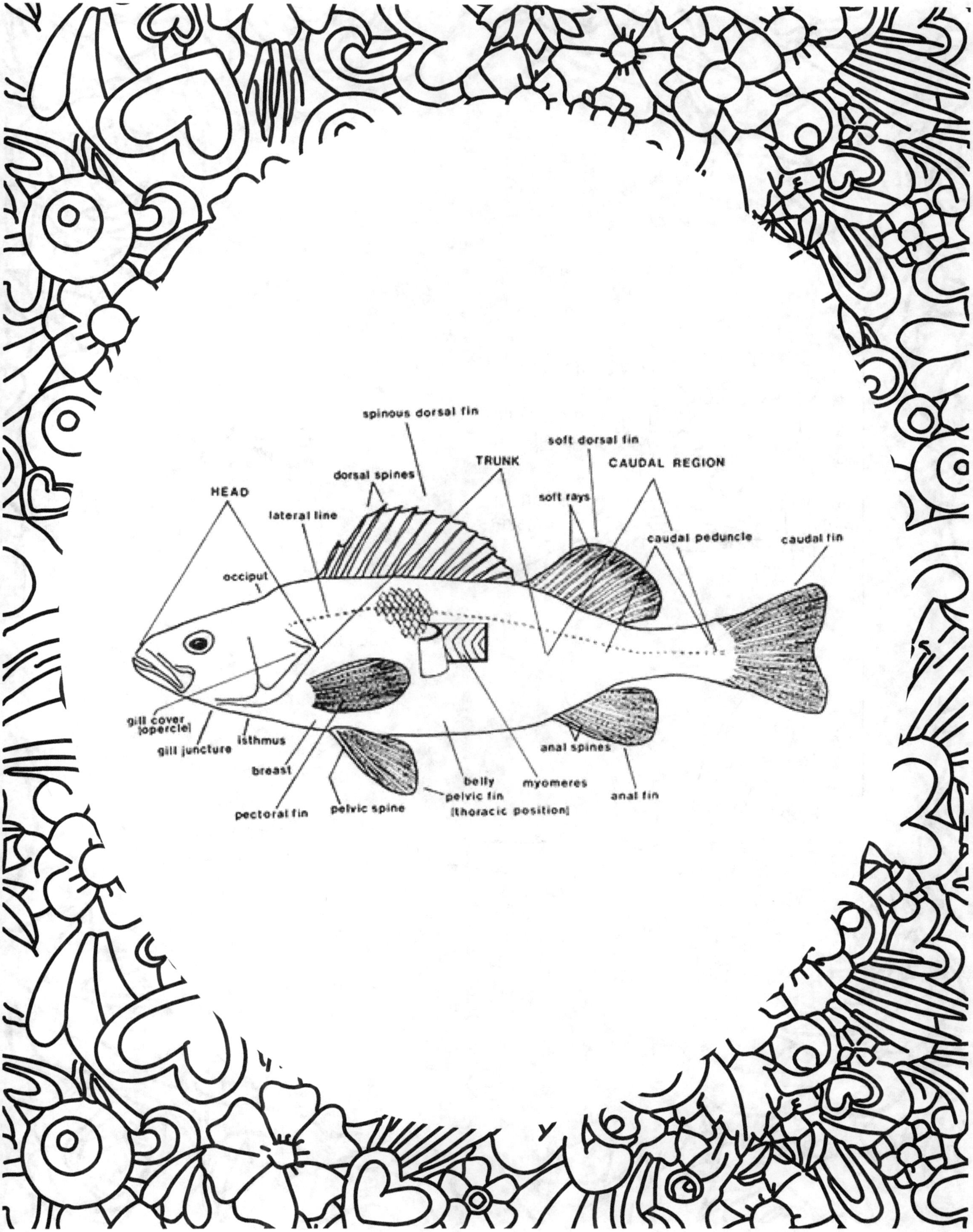
spinous dorsal fin
soft dorsal fin
TRUNK
CAUDAL REGION
dorsal spines
HEAD
soft rays
lateral line
caudal peduncle
caudal fin
occiput
gill cover [opercle]
gill juncture
isthmus
breast
anal spines
belly
myomeres
pelvic fin [thoracic position]
anal fin
pectoral fin
pelvic spine

# Cat

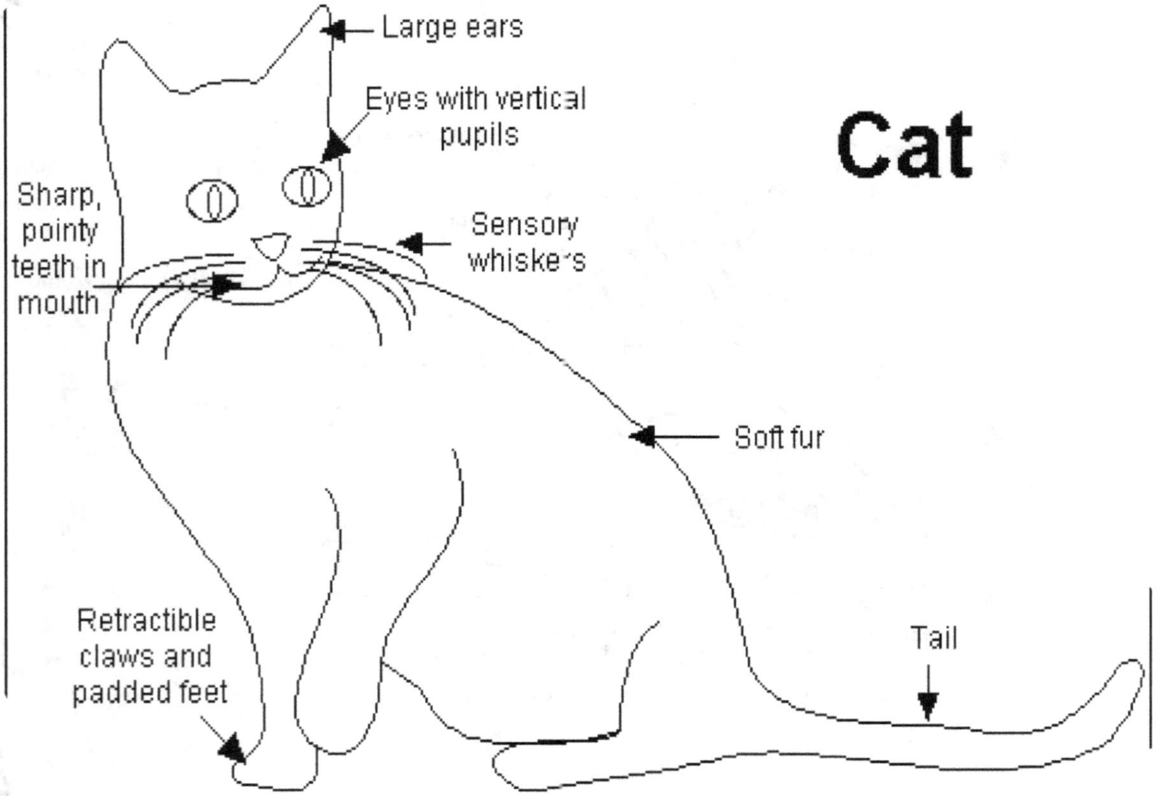
Large ears
Eyes with vertical pupils
Sharp, pointy teeth in mouth
Sensory whiskers
Soft fur
Retractible claws and padded feet
Tail

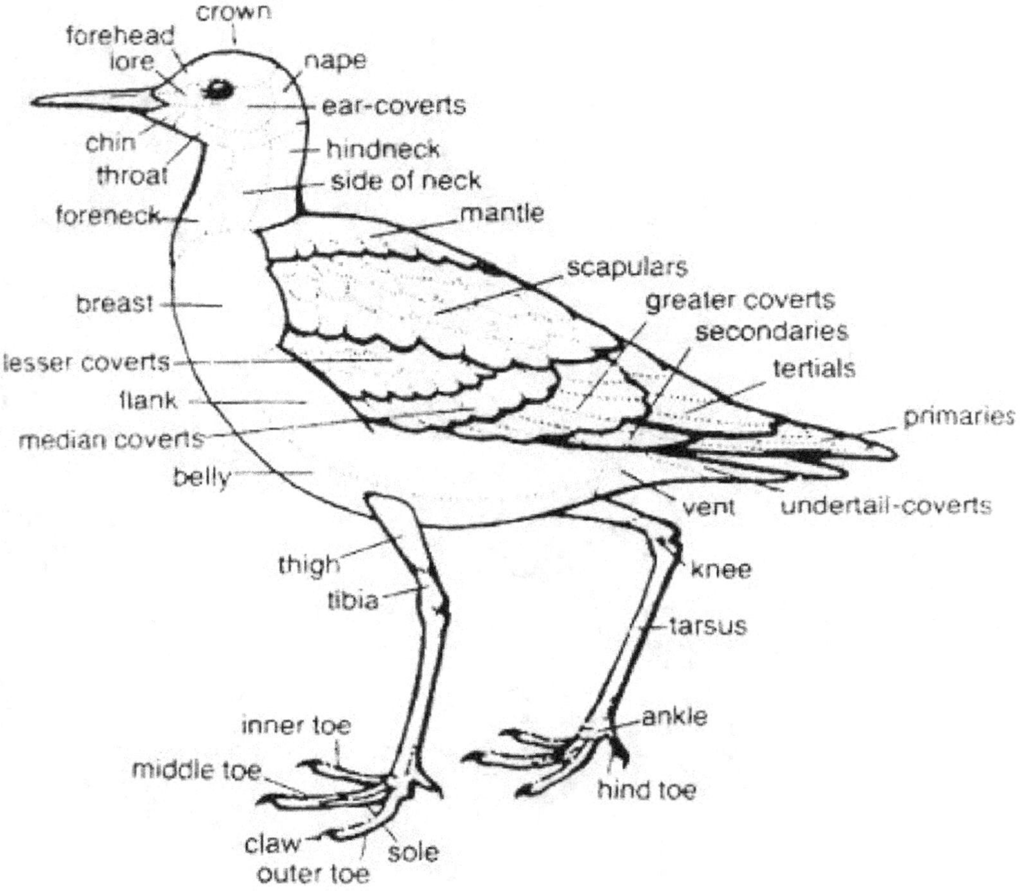
crown
forehead
lore
nape
ear-coverts
chin
hindneck
throat
side of neck
foreneck
mantle
scapulars
breast
greater coverts
secondaries
lesser coverts
tertials
flank
primaries
median coverts
belly
vent
undertail-coverts
thigh
knee
tibia
tarsus
ankle
inner toe
middle toe
hind toe
claw
sole
outer toe

Black bill with light band
Black eye
Black horseshoe shaped stripe
White chest
Black wings that they use in the water like flippers
Black chest speckles
Black webbed feet with some pink and black claws

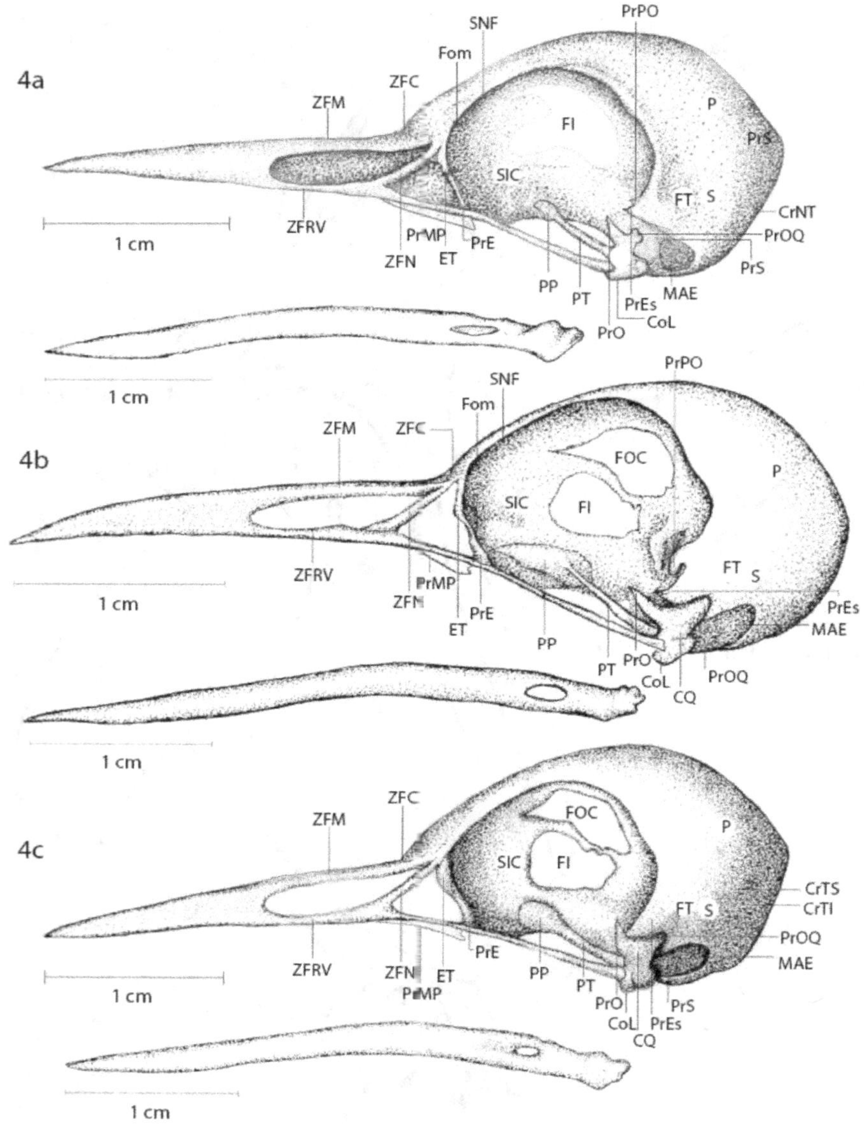
4a
SNF
PrPO
Fom
ZFC
ZFM
FI
P
PrS
SIC
FT
S
CrNT
PrOQ
ZFRV
PrMP
PrE
ZFN
ET
PrS
PP
PT
PrEs
MAE
CoL
PrO
1 cm
1 cm
4b
SNF
PrPO
Fom
ZFM
ZFC
FOC
P
SIC
FI
FT
S
PrEs
MAE
ZFRV
PrMP
ZFN
ET
PrE
PP
PT
PrO
CoL
CQ
PrOQ
1 cm
1 cm
4c
ZFC
ZFM
FOC
P
SIC
FI
CrTS
CrTI
FT
S
PrOQ
MAE
PrE
ZFRV
ZFN
PrMP
ET
PP
PT
PrO
CoL
CQ
PrS
PrEs
1 cm
1 cm

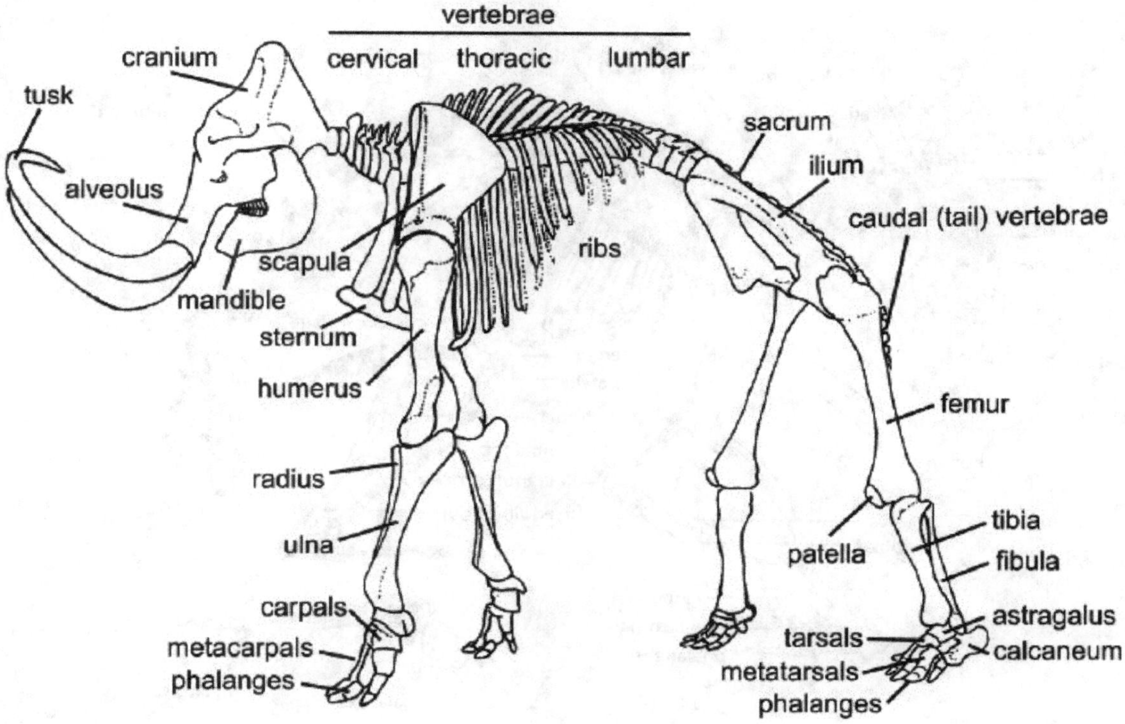
vertebrae
cervical
thoracic
lumbar
cranium
tusk
alveolus
scapula
mandible
sternum
humerus
radius
ulna
carpals
metacarpals
phalanges
ribs
sacrum
ilium
caudal (tail) vertebrae
femur
patella
tibia
fibula
astragalus
tarsals
calcaneum
metatarsals
phalanges

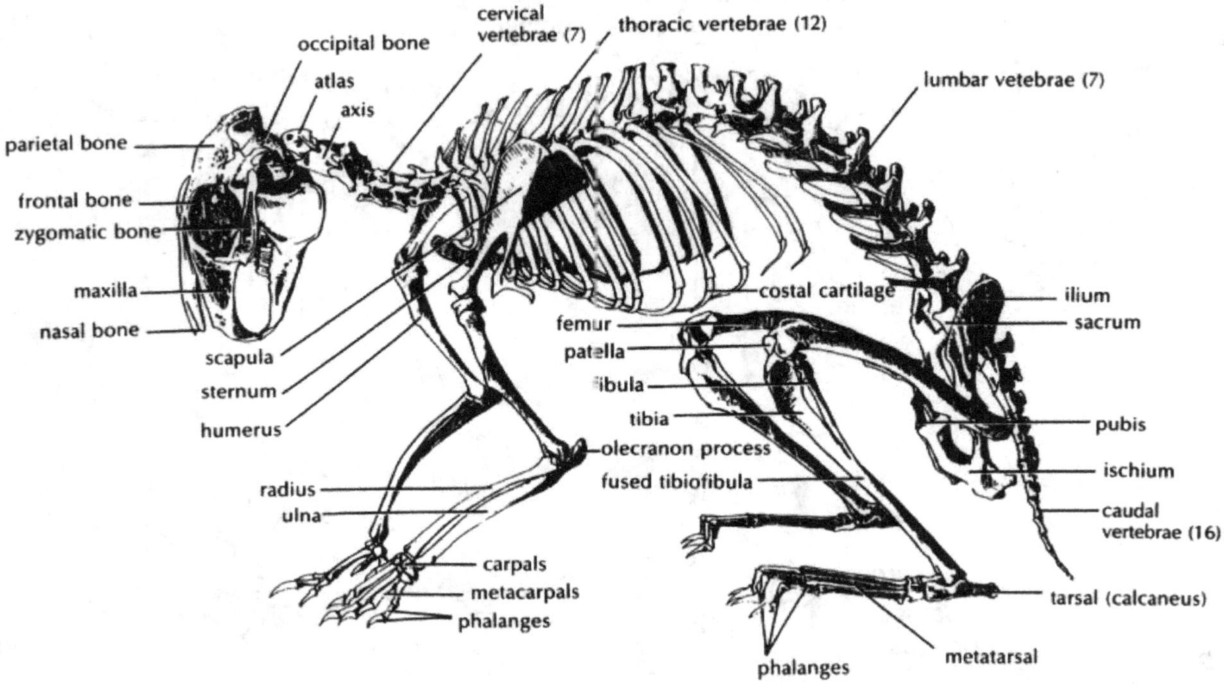

occipital bone
cervical vertebrae (7)
thoracic vertebrae (12)
atlas
axis
lumbar vetebrae (7)
parietal bone
frontal bone
zygomatic bone
maxilla
nasal bone
scapula
sternum
humerus
costal cartilage
ilium
sacrum
femur
patella
fibula
tibia
pubis
olecranon process
ischium
radius
fused tibiofibula
ulna
caudal vertebrae (16)
carpals
metacarpals
phalanges
tarsal (calcaneus)
metatarsal
phalanges

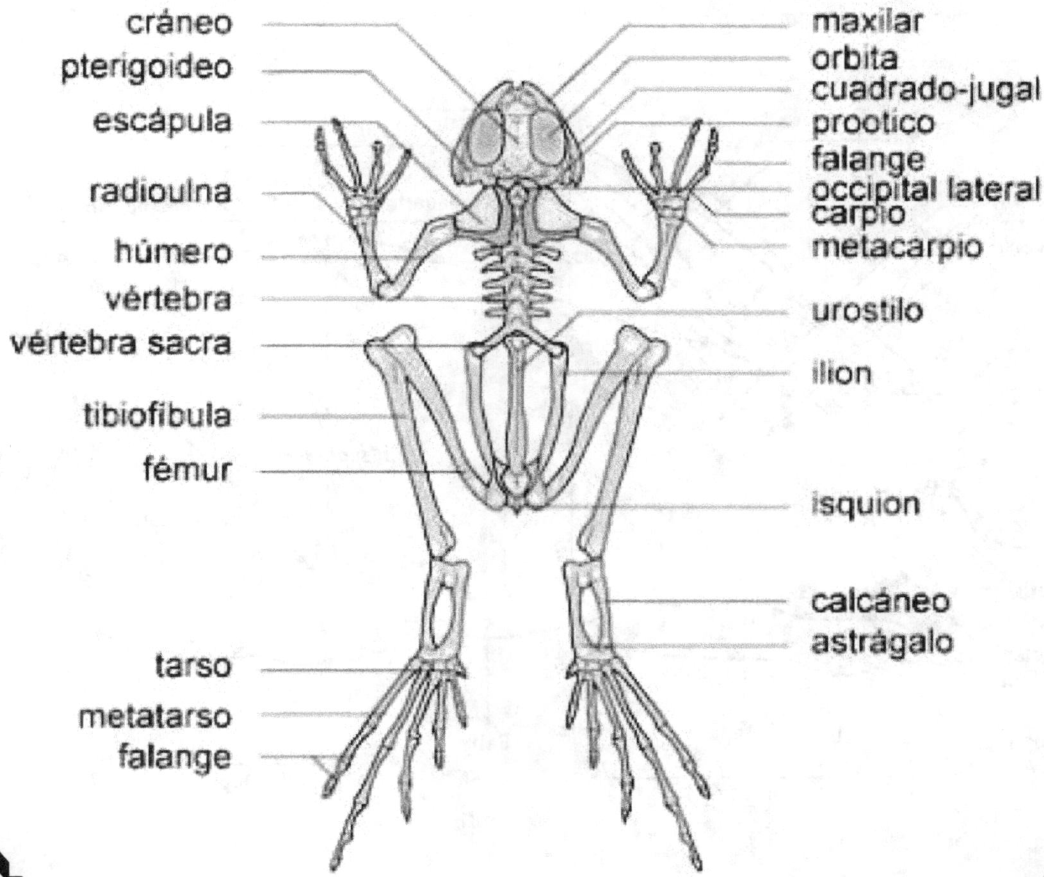
cráneo
pterigoideo
escápula
radioulna
húmero
vértebra
vértebra sacra
tibiofíbula
fémur
tarso
metatarso
falange
maxilar
orbita
cuadrado-jugal
prootico
falange
occipital lateral
carpio
metacarpio
urostilo
ilion
isquion
calcáneo
astrágalo

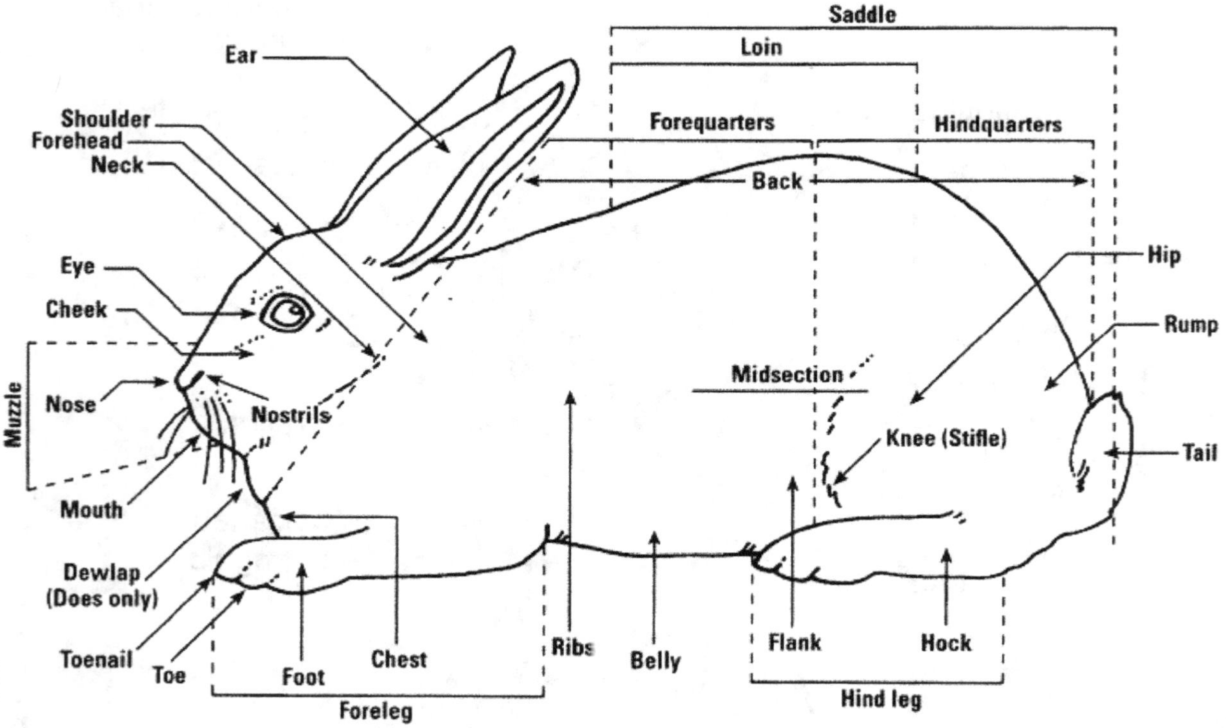
Saddle
Loin
Ear
Shoulder
Forehead
Neck
Forequarters
Hindquarters
Back
Eye
Hip
Cheek
Rump
Muzzle
Midsection
Nose
Nostrils
Knee (Stifle)
Tail
Mouth
Dewlap
(Does only)
Toenail
Toe
Foot
Chest
Ribs
Belly
Flank
Hock
Foreleg
Hind leg

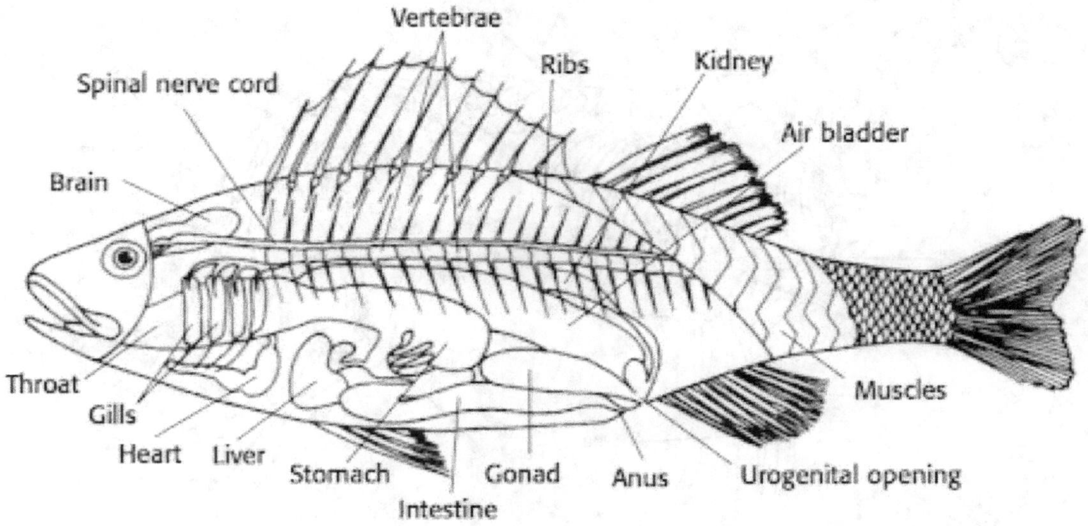

Vertebrae
Ribs
Kidney
Spinal nerve cord
Air bladder
Brain
Throat
Gills
Heart
Liver
Stomach
Intestine
Gonad
Anus
Urogenital opening
Muscles

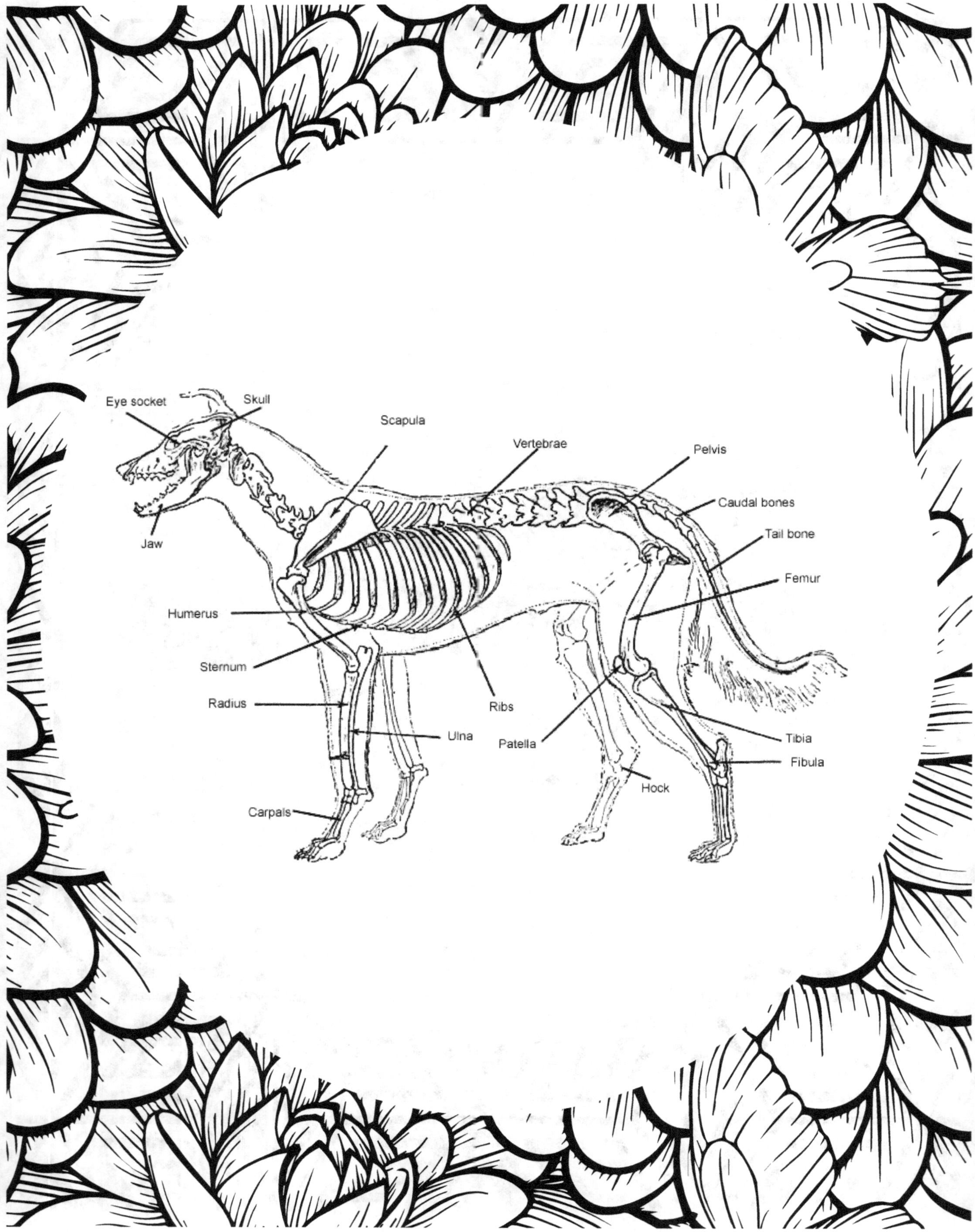
Eye socket
Skull
Scapula
Vertebrae
Pelvis
Caudal bones
Tail bone
Femur
Jaw
Humerus
Sternum
Radius
Ribs
Ulna
Patella
Tibia
Fibula
Hock
Carpals

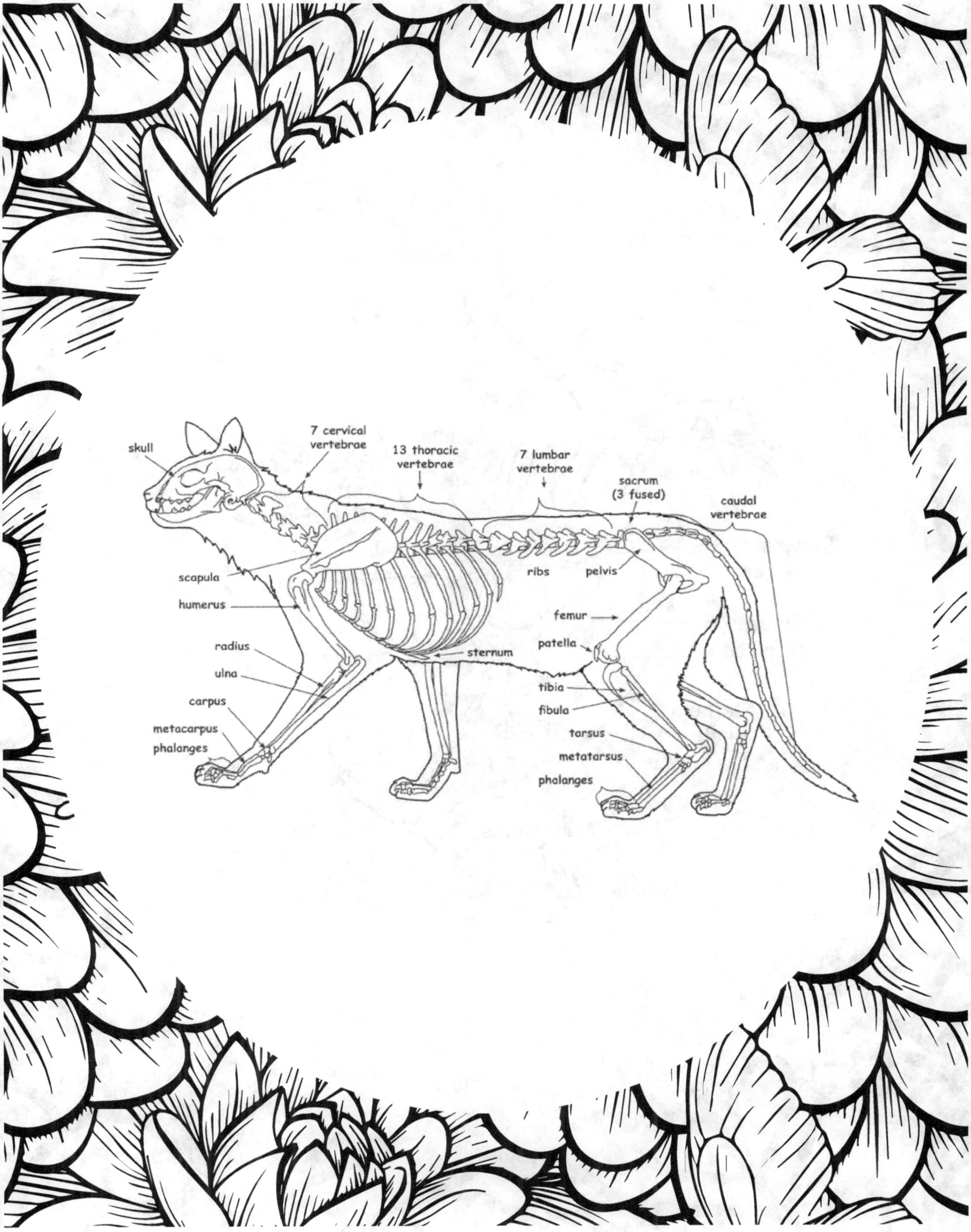

skull
7 cervical vertebrae
13 thoracic vertebrae
7 lumbar vertebrae
sacrum (3 fused)
caudal vertebrae
scapula
ribs
pelvis
humerus
femur
radius
sternum
patella
ulna
tibia
carpus
fibula
metacarpus
tarsus
phalanges
metatarsus
phalanges

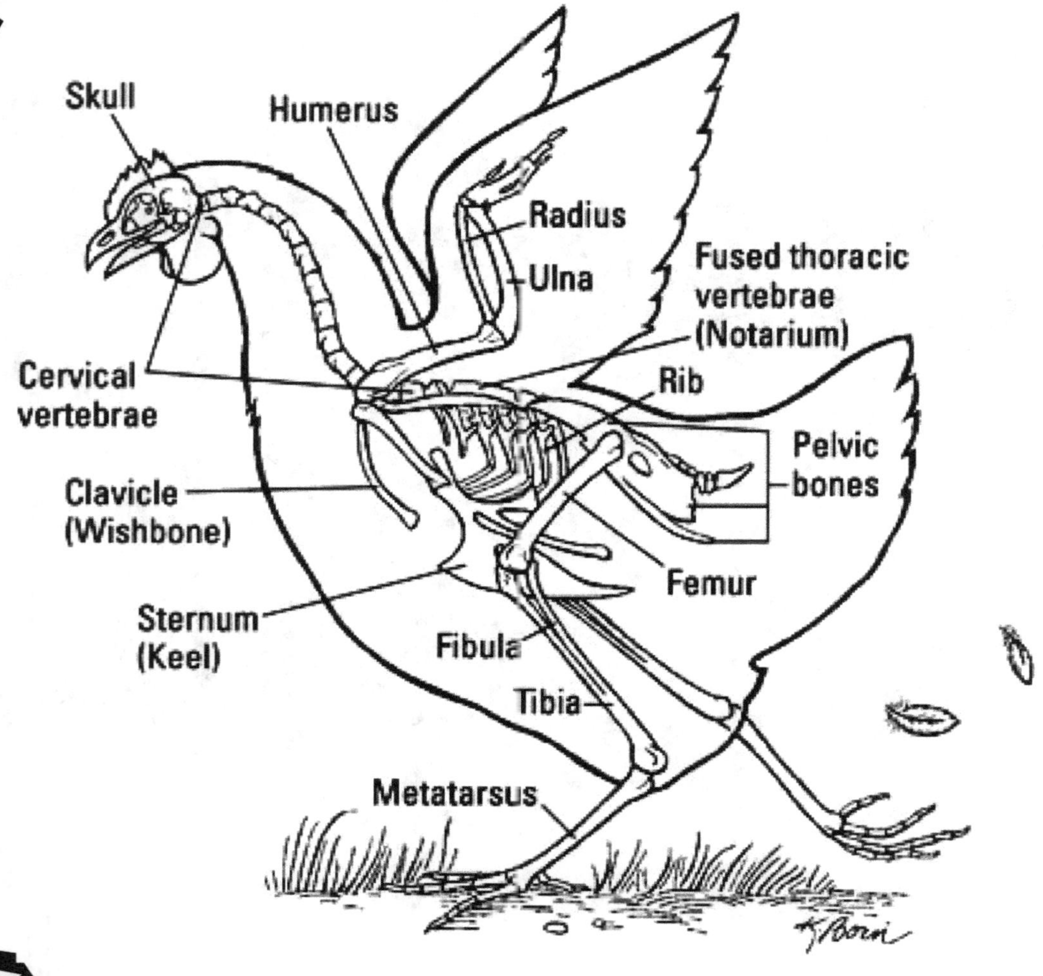
Skull
Humerus
Radius
Ulna
Fused thoracic vertebrae (Notarium)
Cervical vertebrae
Rib
Pelvic bones
Clavicle (Wishbone)
Femur
Sternum (Keel)
Fibula
Tibia
Metatarsus

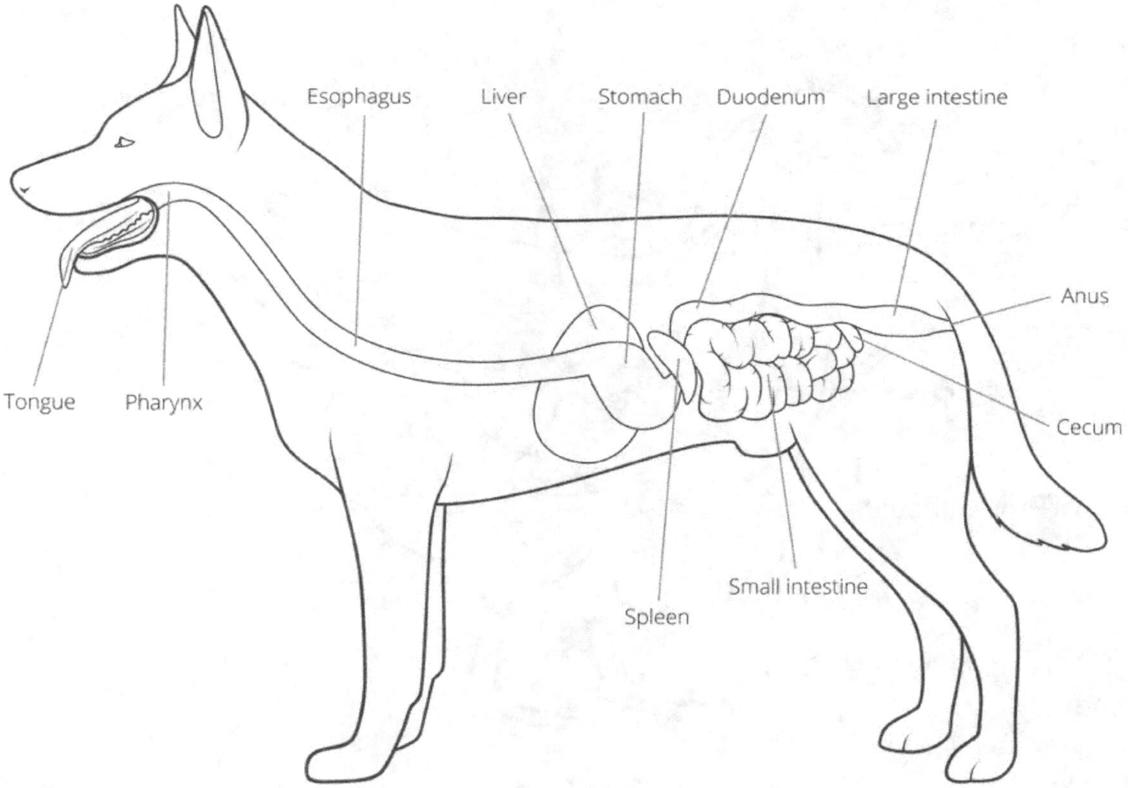
Esophagus
Liver
Stomach
Duodenum
Large intestine
Anus
Cecum
Tongue
Pharynx
Small intestine
Spleen

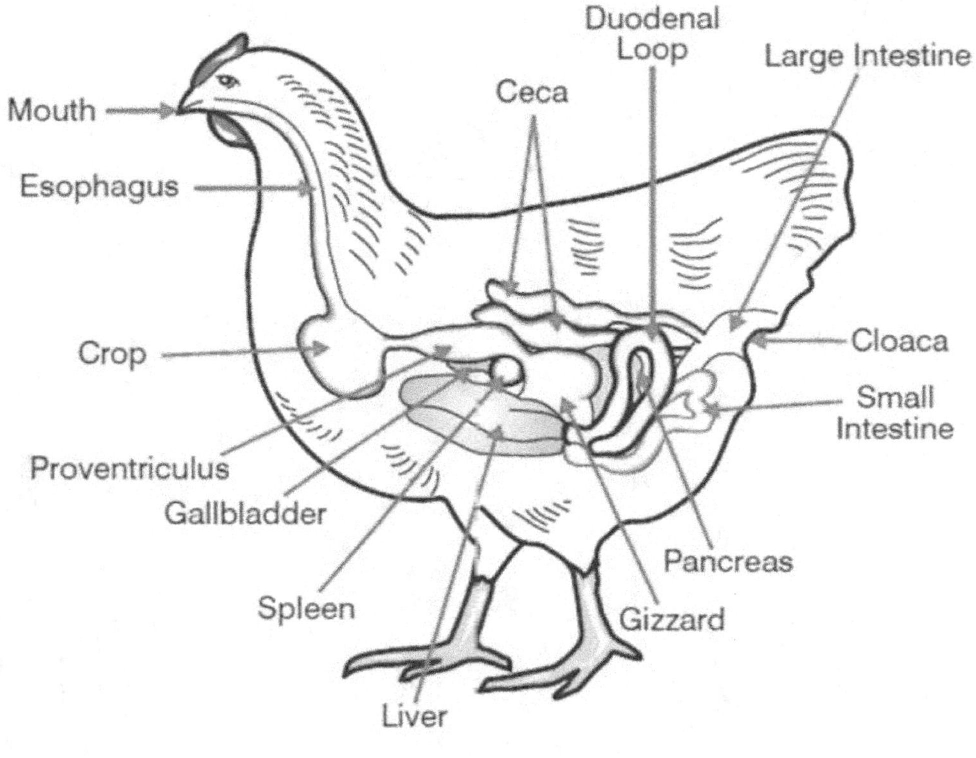
Duodenal
Loop
Large Intestine
Ceca
Mouth
Esophagus
Cloaca
Crop
Small
Intestine
Proventriculus
Gallbladder
Pancreas
Spleen
Gizzard
Liver

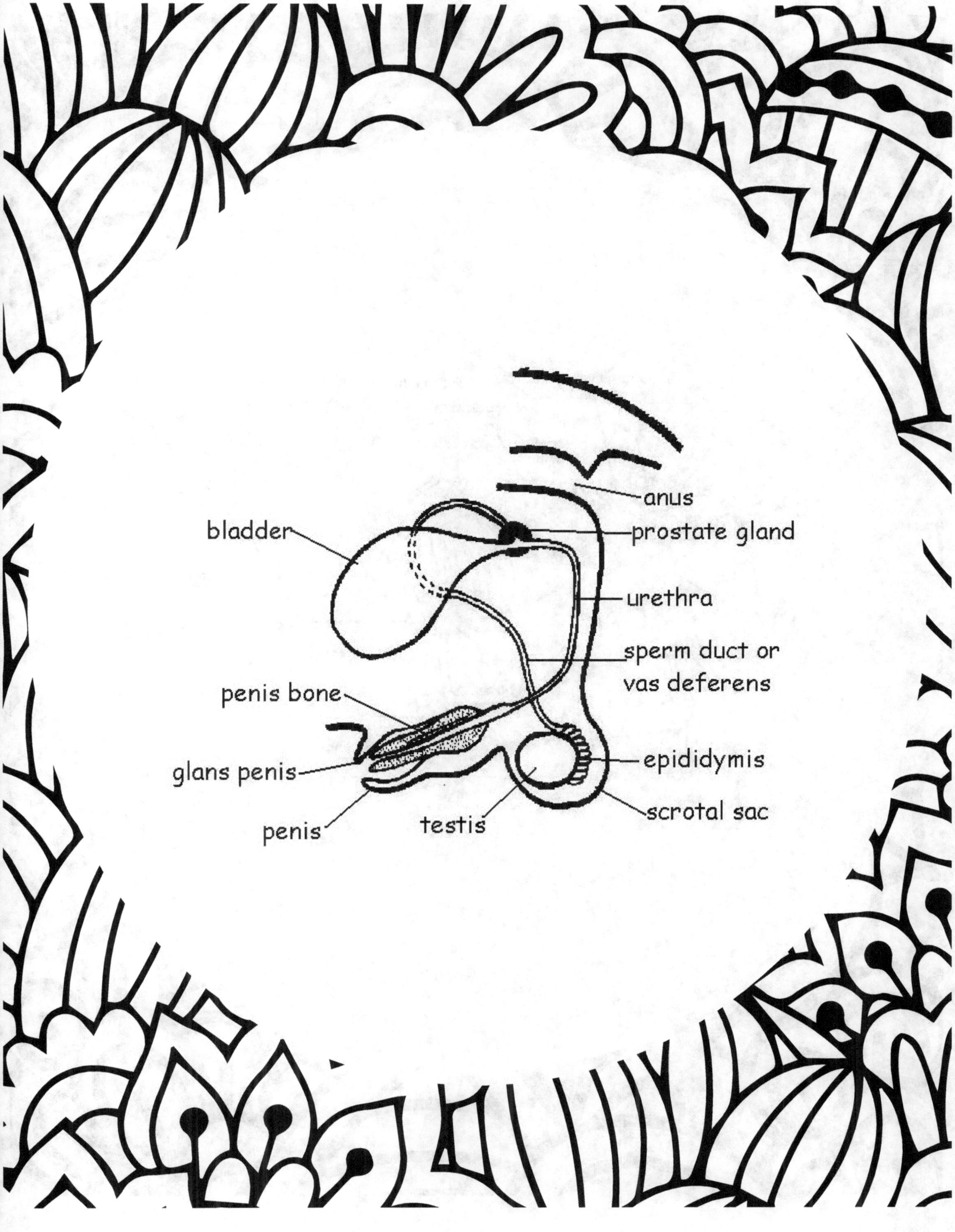
anus
bladder
prostate gland
urethra
sperm duct or
vas deferens
penis bone
glans penis
epididymis
penis
testis
scrotal sac

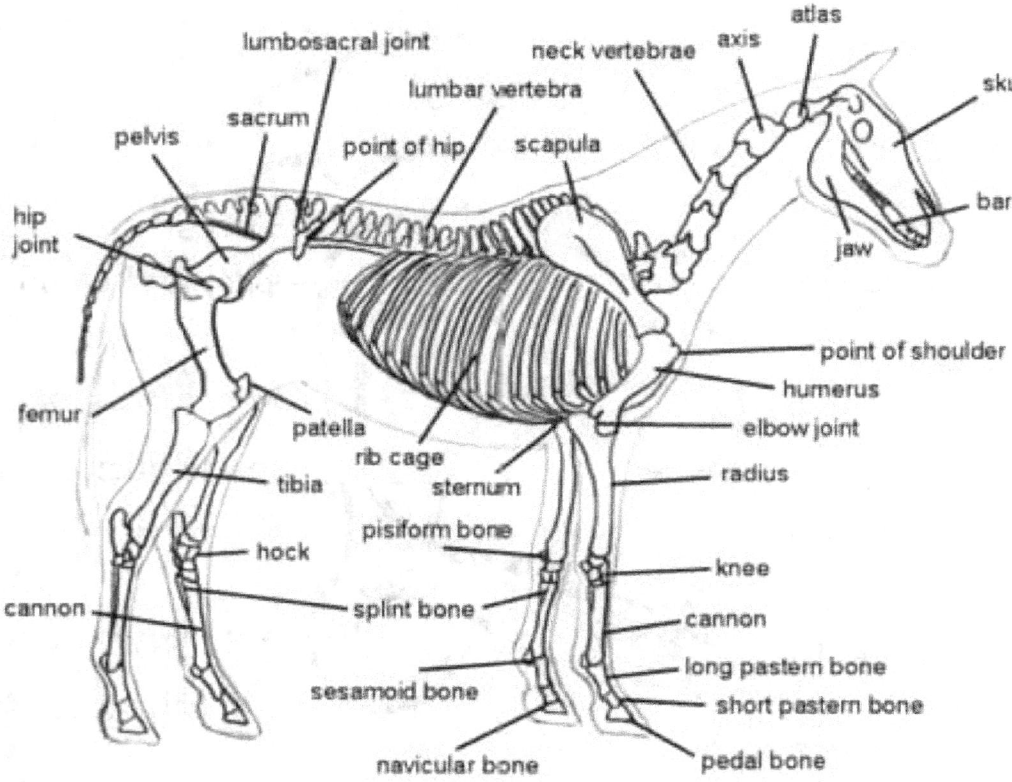
lumbosacral joint
atlas
axis
neck vertebrae
skull
lumbar vertebra
sacrum
pelvis
point of hip
scapula
bars
hip
joint
jaw
point of shoulder
humerus
femur
patella
elbow joint
rib cage
radius
tibia
sternum
pisiform bone
hock
knee
cannon
splint bone
cannon
long pastern bone
sesamoid bone
short pastern bone
pedal bone
navicular bone

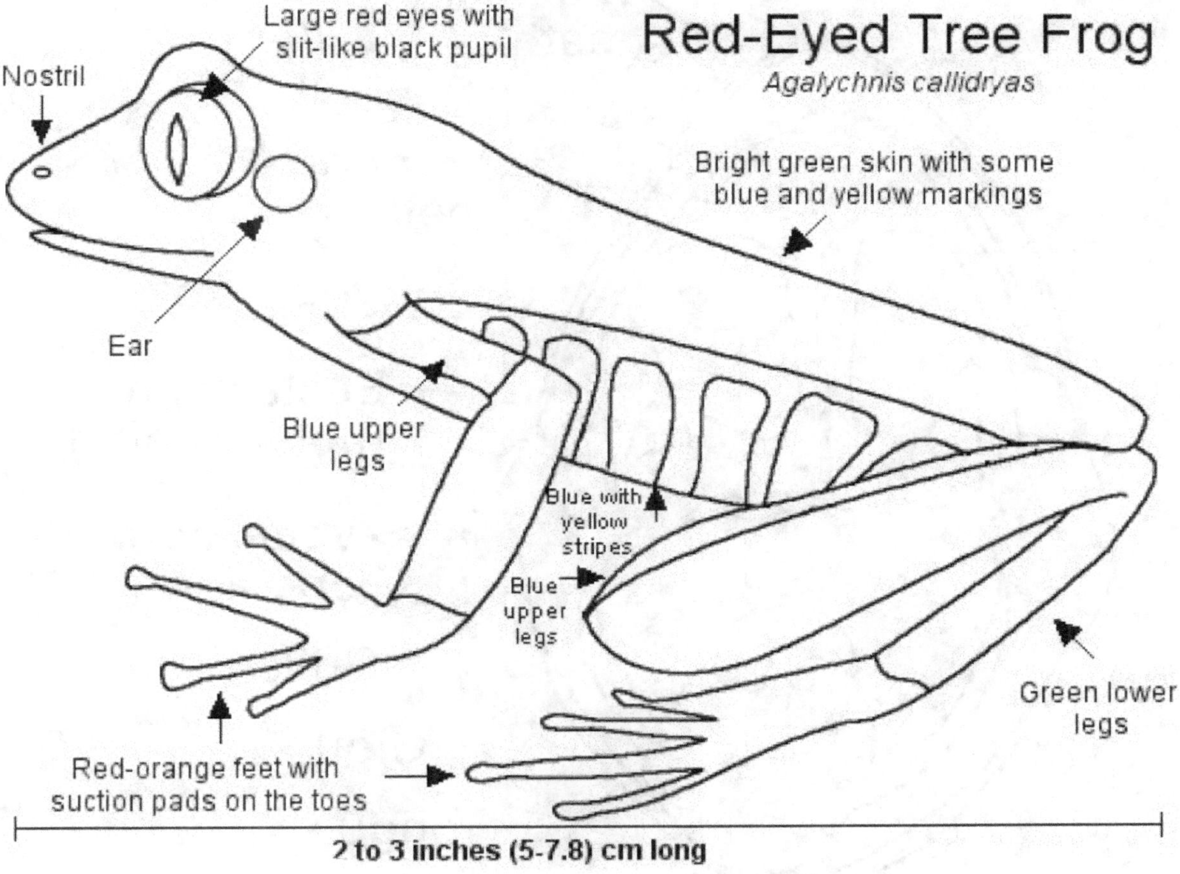
Red-Eyed Tree Frog
Agalychnis callidryas
Large red eyes with slit-like black pupil
Nostril
Bright green skin with some blue and yellow markings
Ear
Blue upper legs
Blue with yellow stripes
Blue upper legs
Green lower legs
Red-orange feet with suction pads on the toes
2 to 3 inches (5-7.8) cm long

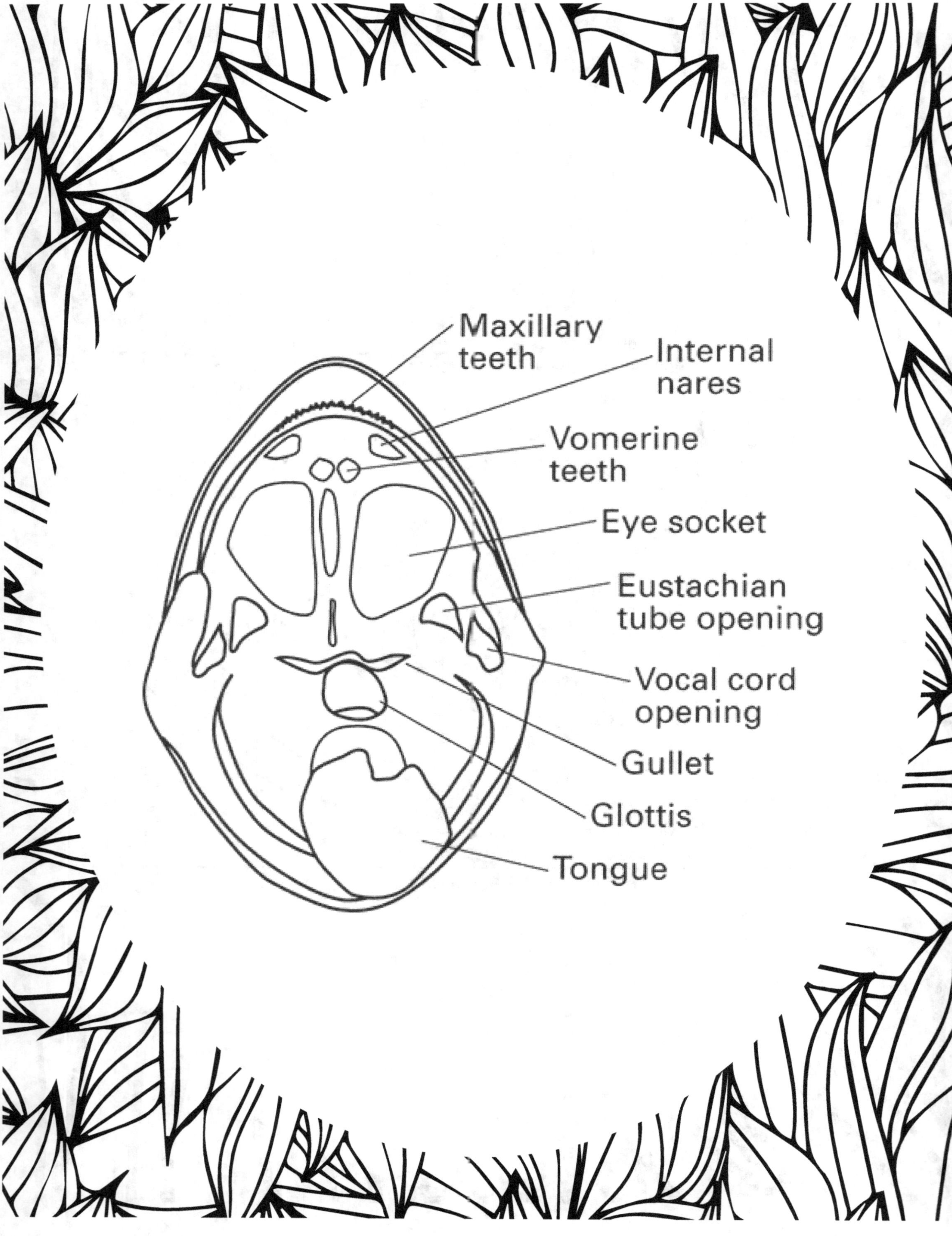
Maxillary teeth
Internal nares
Vomerine teeth
Eye socket
Eustachian tube opening
Vocal cord opening
Gullet
Glottis
Tongue

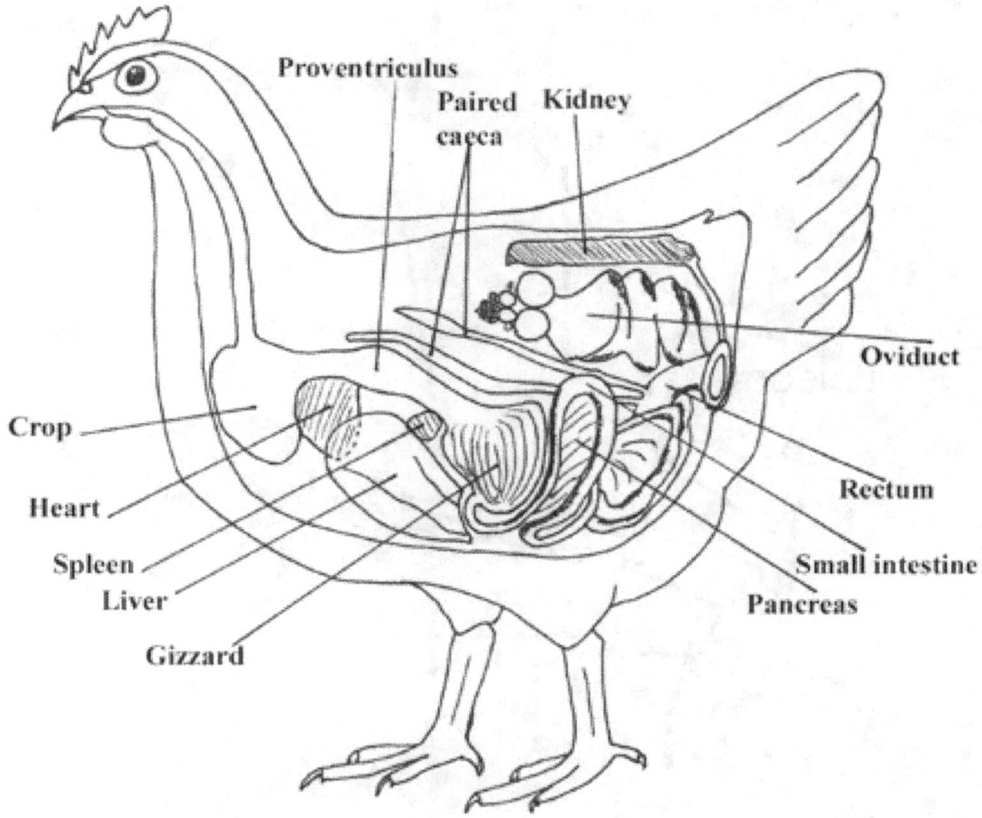
Proventriculus
Paired caeca
Kidney
Oviduct
Crop
Heart
Spleen
Liver
Gizzard
Rectum
Small intestine
Pancreas

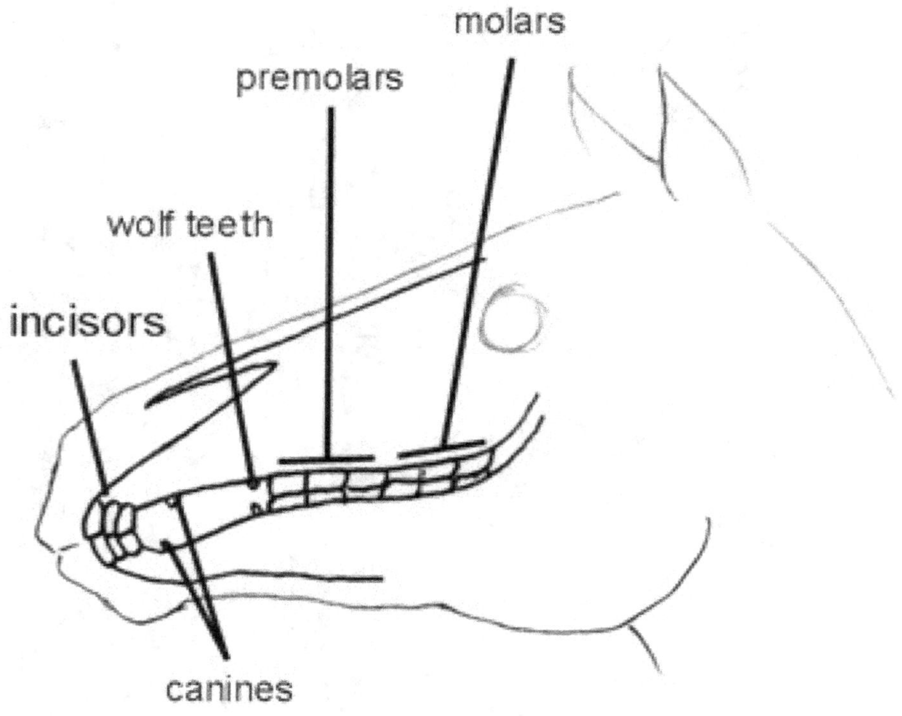
molars
premolars
wolf teeth
incisors
canines

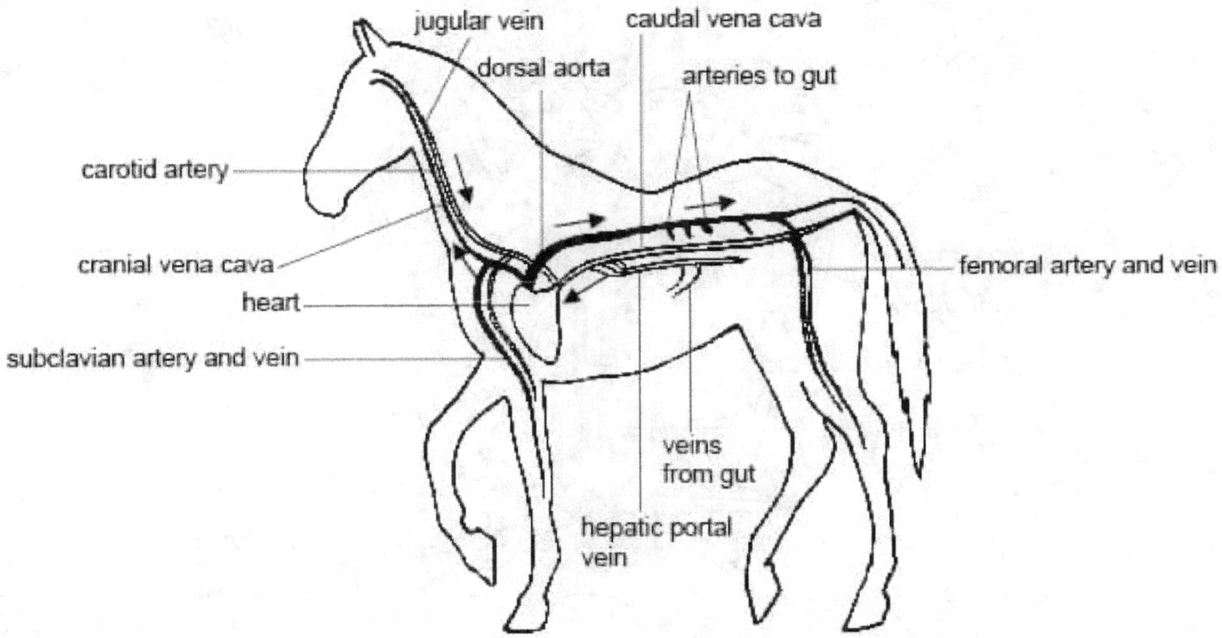
jugular vein
caudal vena cava
dorsal aorta
arteries to gut
carotid artery
cranial vena cava
femoral artery and vein
heart
subclavian artery and vein
veins
from gut
hepatic portal
vein

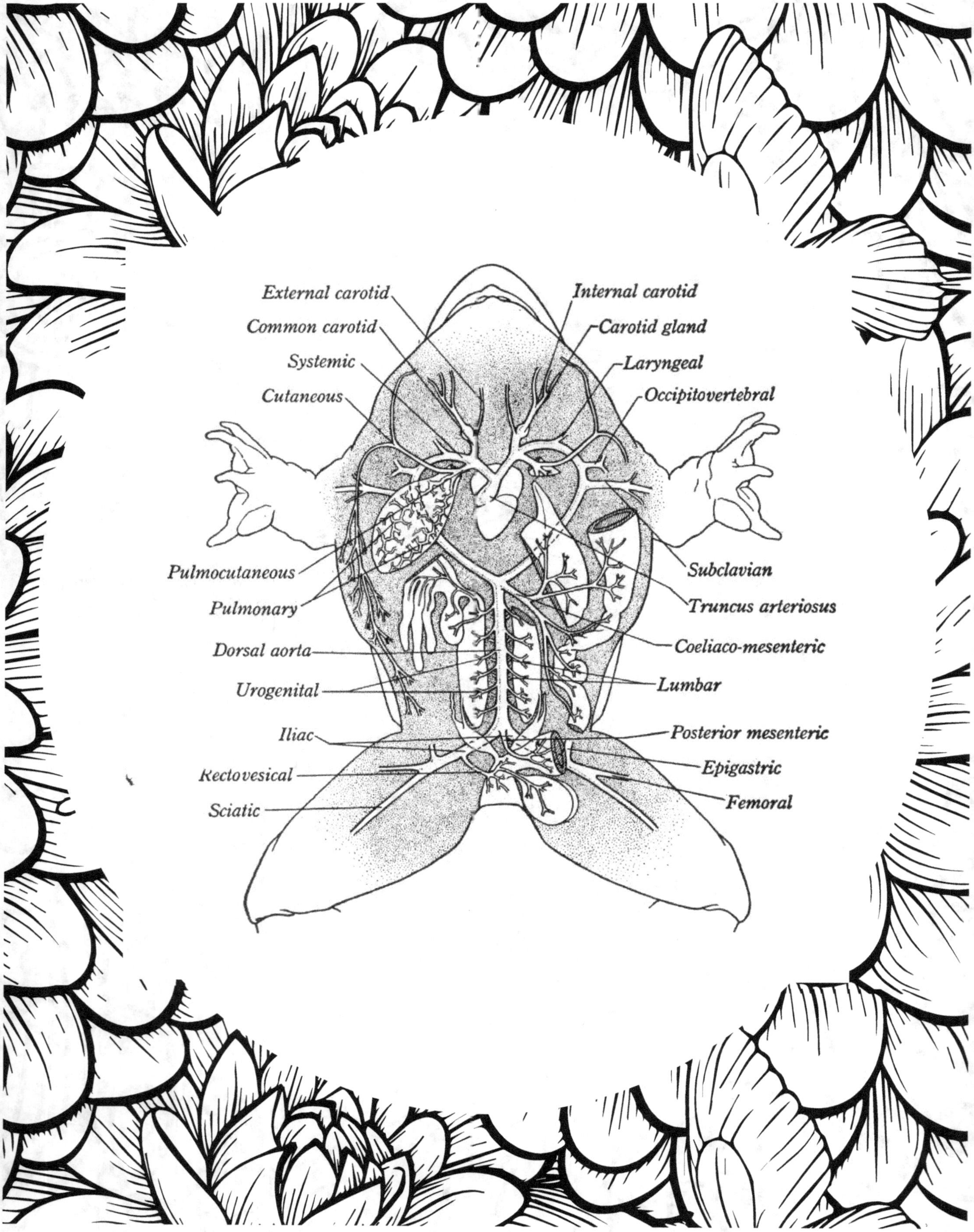
External carotid
Internal carotid
Common carotid
Carotid gland
Systemic
Laryngeal
Cutaneous
Occipitovertebral
Pulmocutaneous
Subclavian
Pulmonary
Truncus arteriosus
Dorsal aorta
Coeliaco-mesenteric
Urogenital
Lumbar
Iliac
Posterior mesenteric
Rectovesical
Epigastric
Sciatic
Femoral

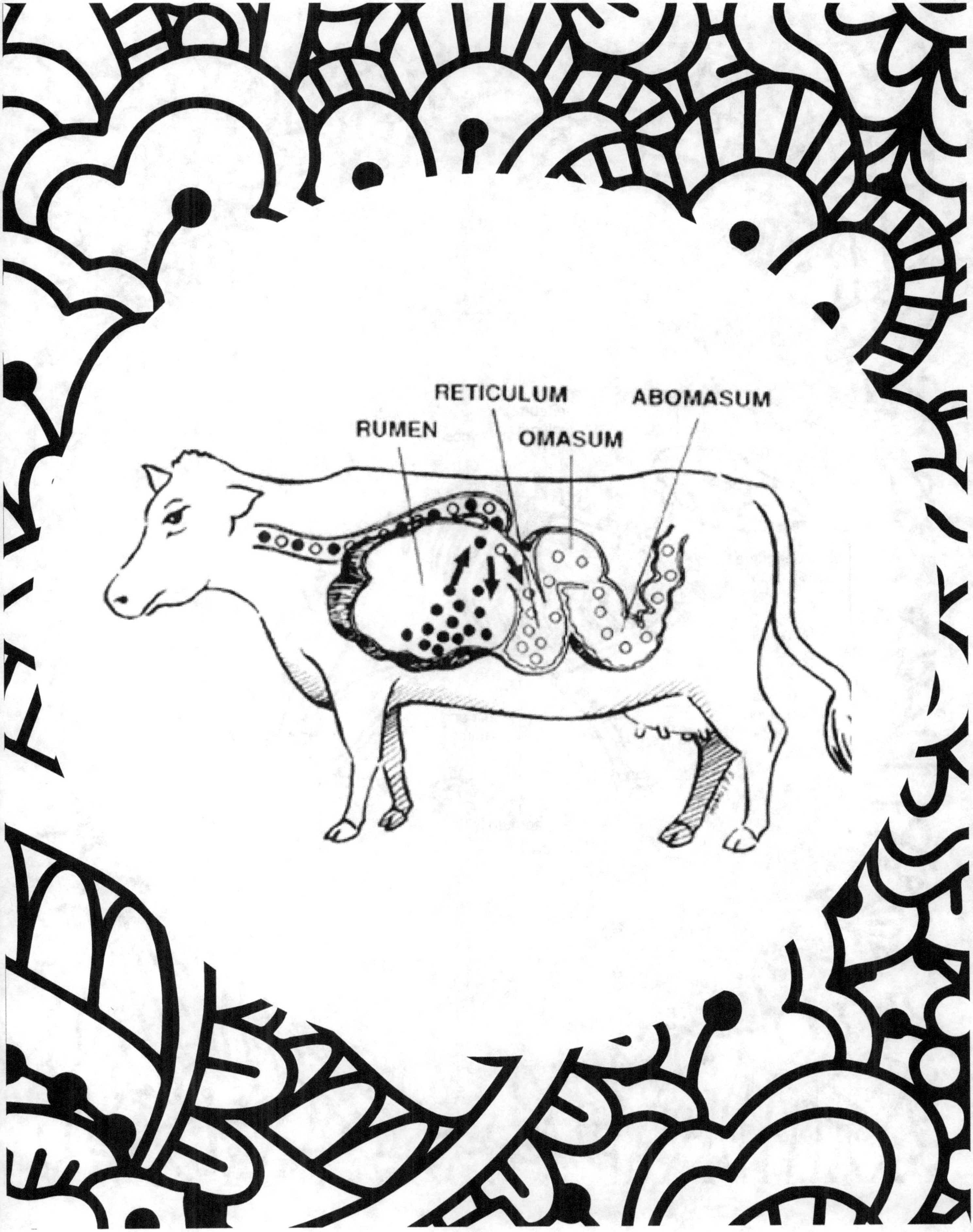
RETICULUM
ABOMASUM
RUMEN
OMASUM

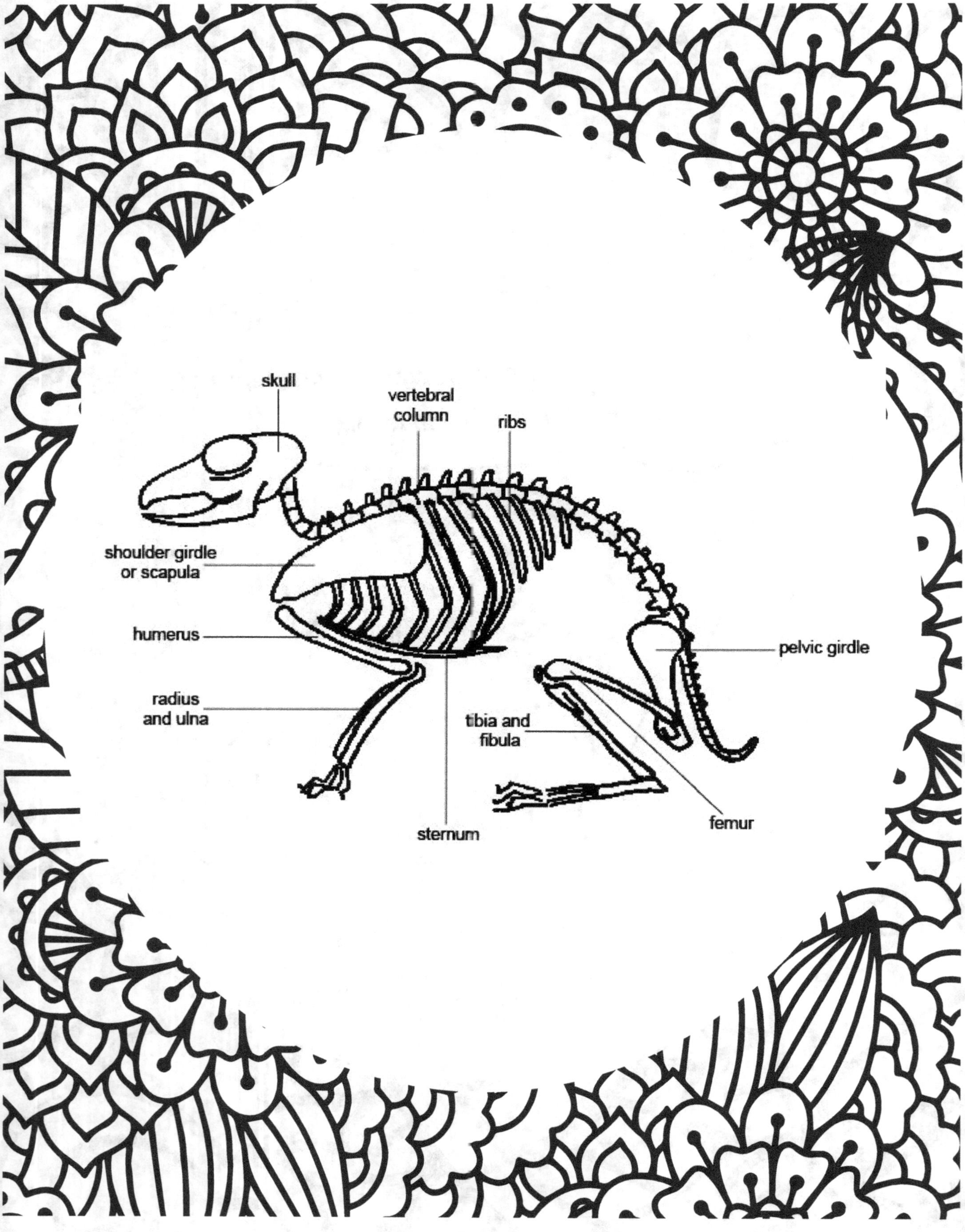
skull
vertebral column
ribs
shoulder girdle or scapula
humerus
radius and ulna
pelvic girdle
tibia and fibula
femur
sternum

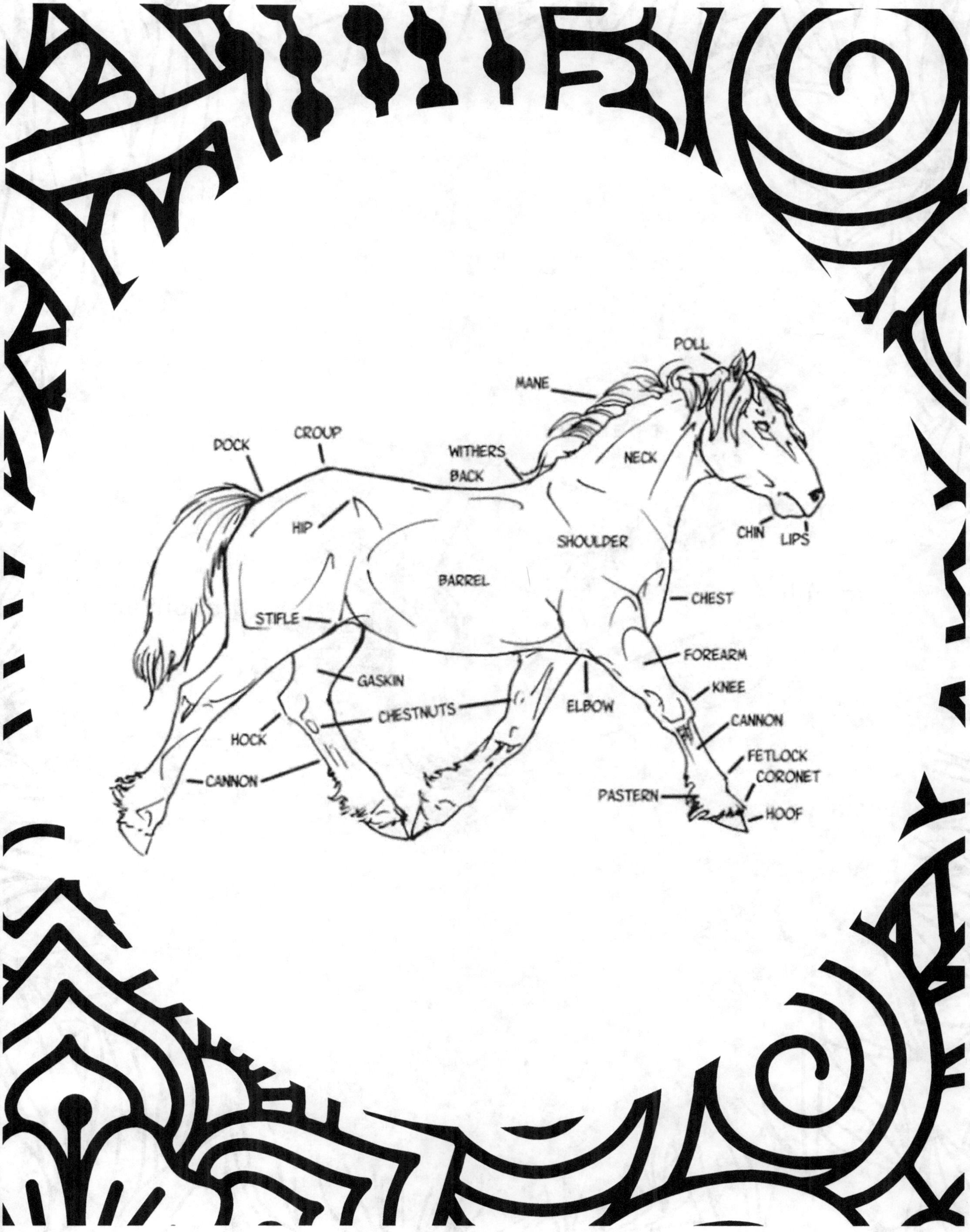
POLL
MANE
DOCK
CROUP
WITHERS
BACK
NECK
HIP
SHOULDER
CHIN
LIPS
BARREL
CHEST
STIFLE
FOREARM
GASKIN
KNEE
CHESTNUTS
ELBOW
CANNON
HOCK
FETLOCK
CANNON
CORONET
PASTERN
HOOF

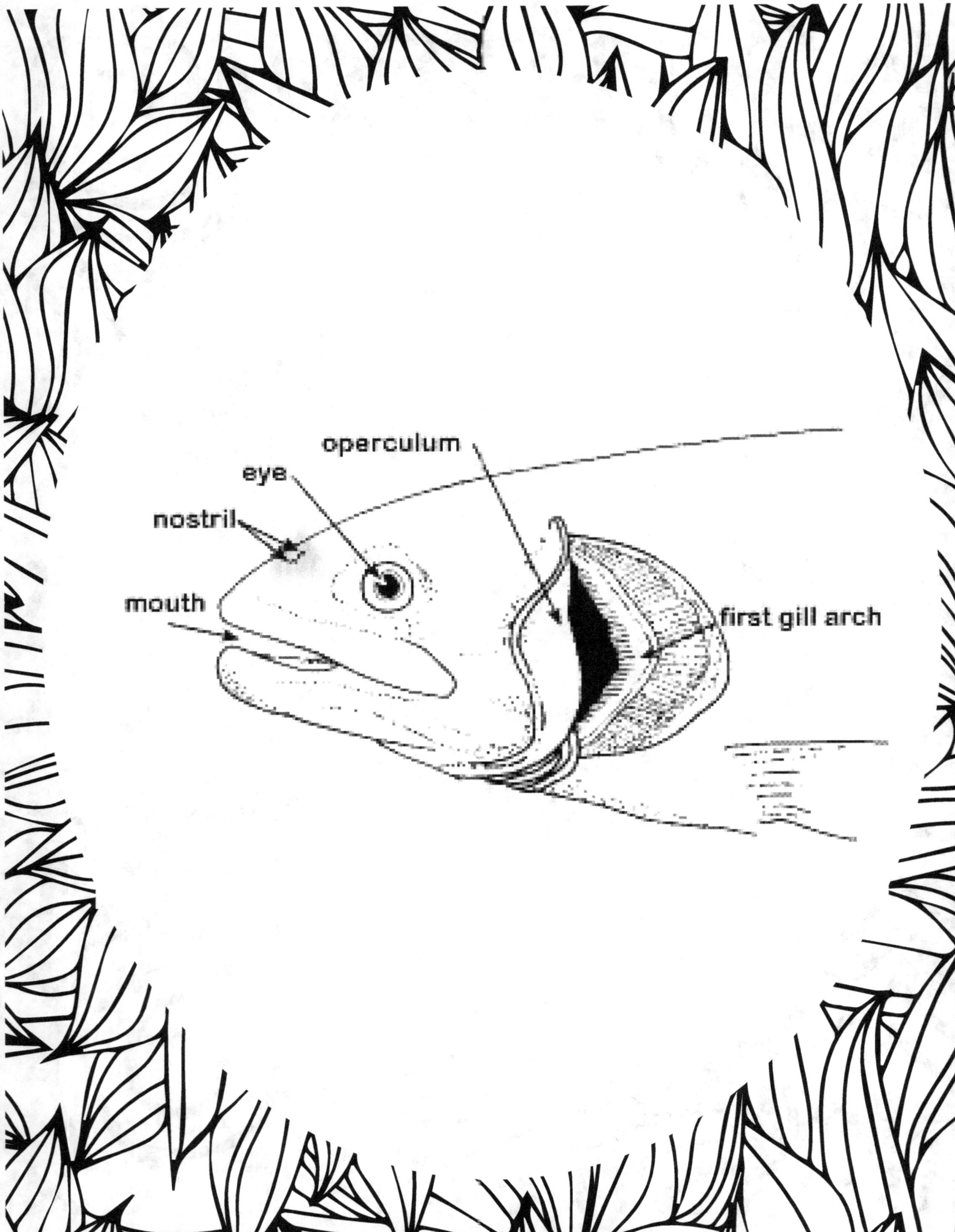
operculum
eye
nostril
mouth
first gill arch

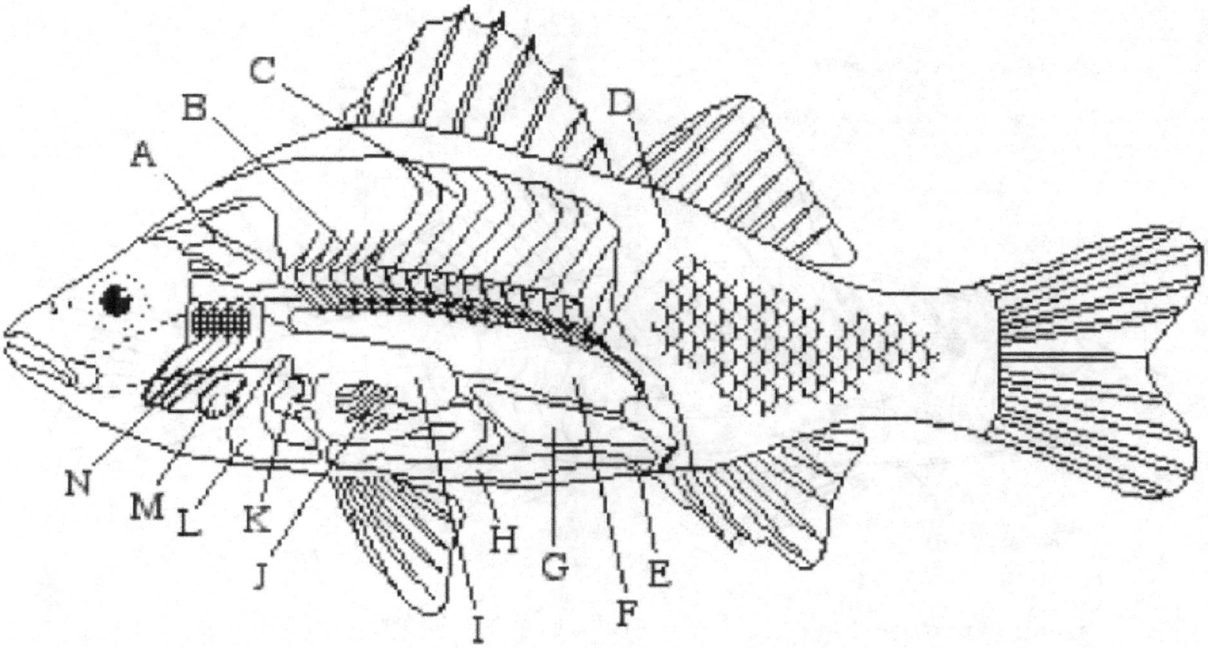
A
B
C
D
E
F
G
H
I
J
K
L
M
N

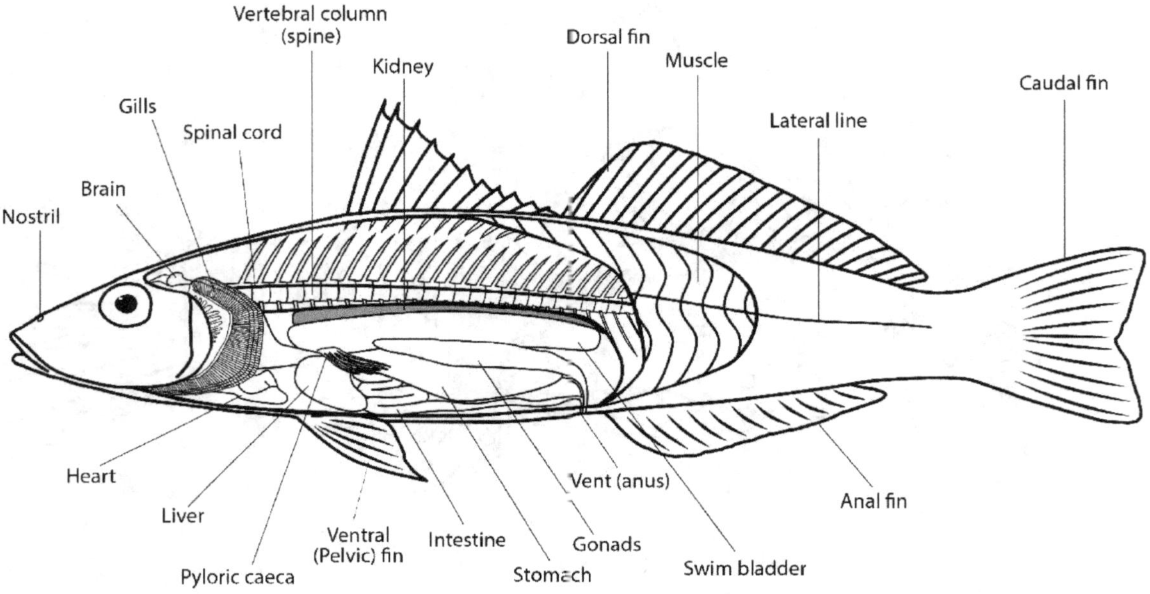
Vertebral column
(spine)
Dorsal fin
Muscle
Kidney
Caudal fin
Gills
Spinal cord
Lateral line
Brain
Nostril
Heart
Liver
Ventral
(Pelvic) fin
Intestine
Vent (anus)
Gonads
Anal fin
Pyloric caeca
Stomach
Swim bladder

# ANATOMY OF A DOG PAW

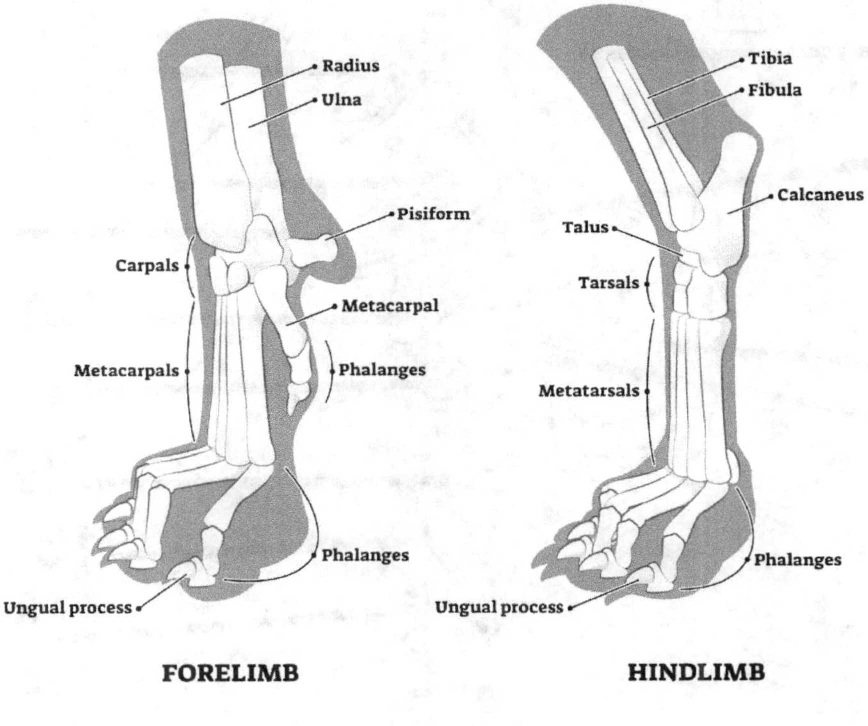

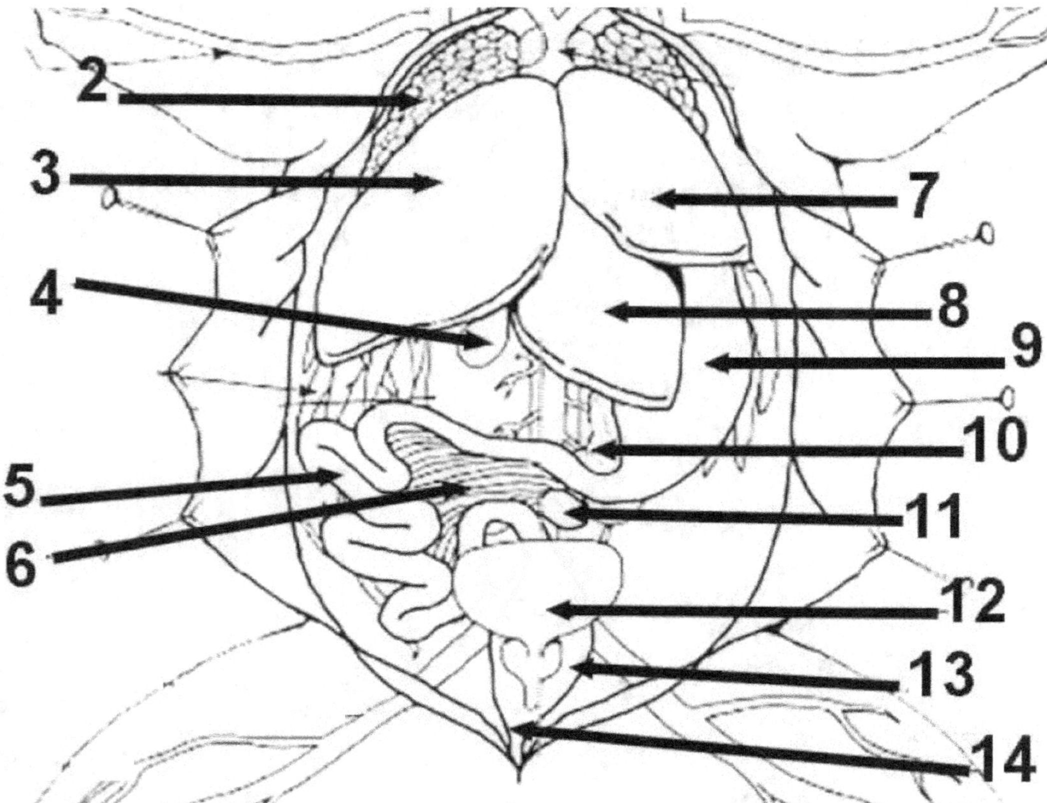
2
3
4
5
6
7
8
9
10
11
12
13
14

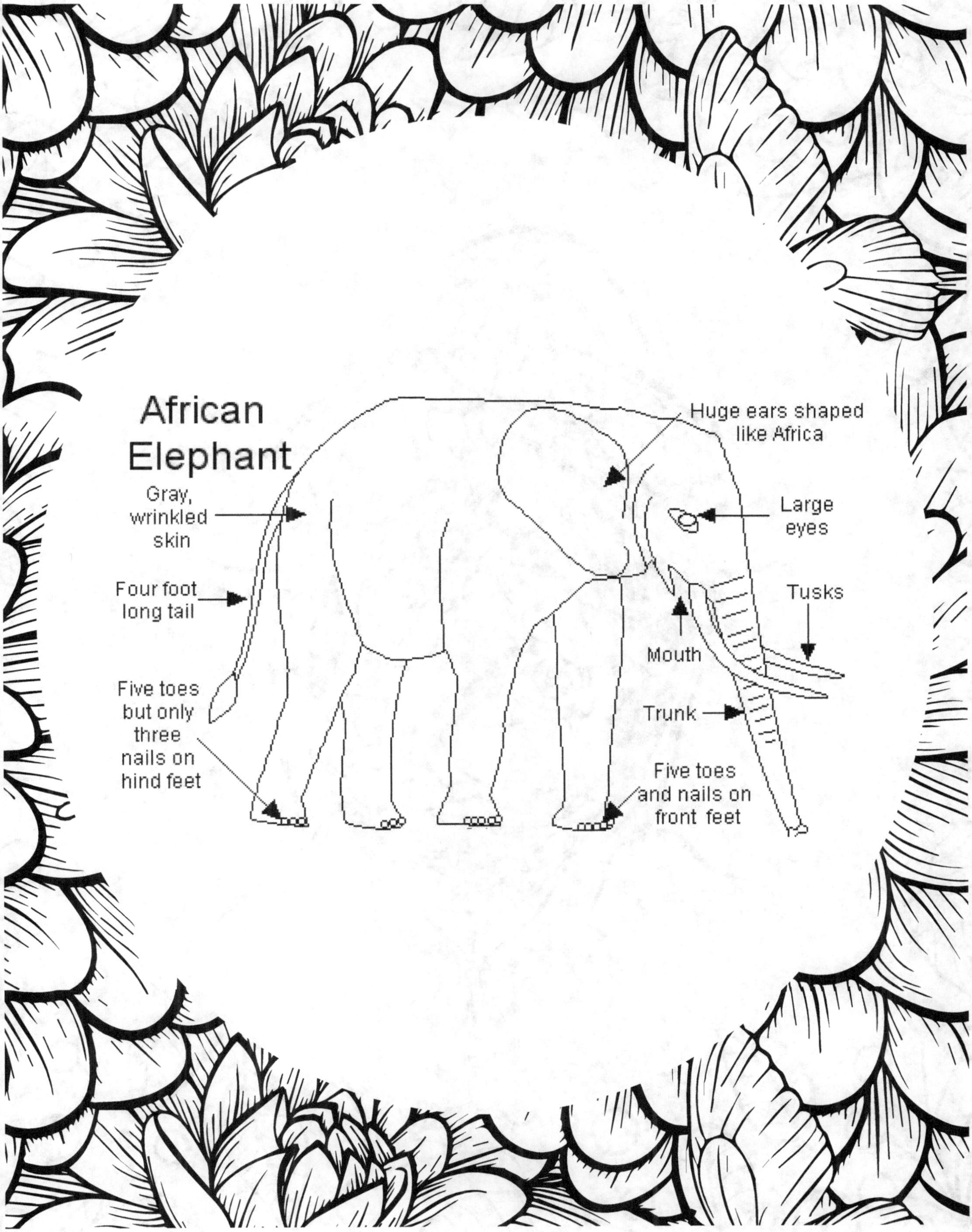
African
Elephant
Huge ears shaped
like Africa
Gray,
wrinkled
skin
Large
eyes
Four foot
long tail
Tusks
Mouth
Five toes
but only
three
nails on
hind feet
Trunk
Five toes
and nails on
front feet

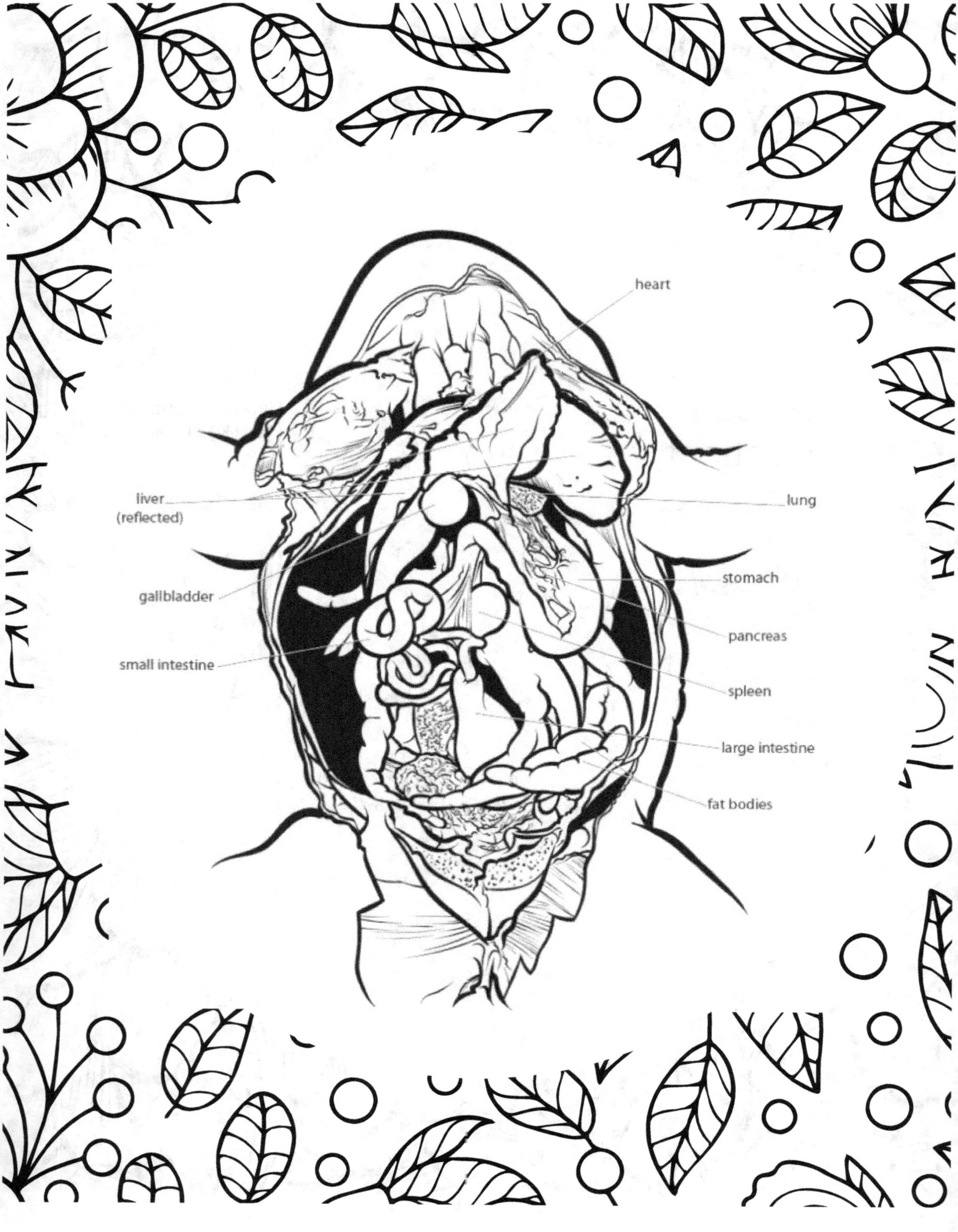
heart
liver
(reflected)
lung
gallbladder
stomach
pancreas
small intestine
spleen
large intestine
fat bodies

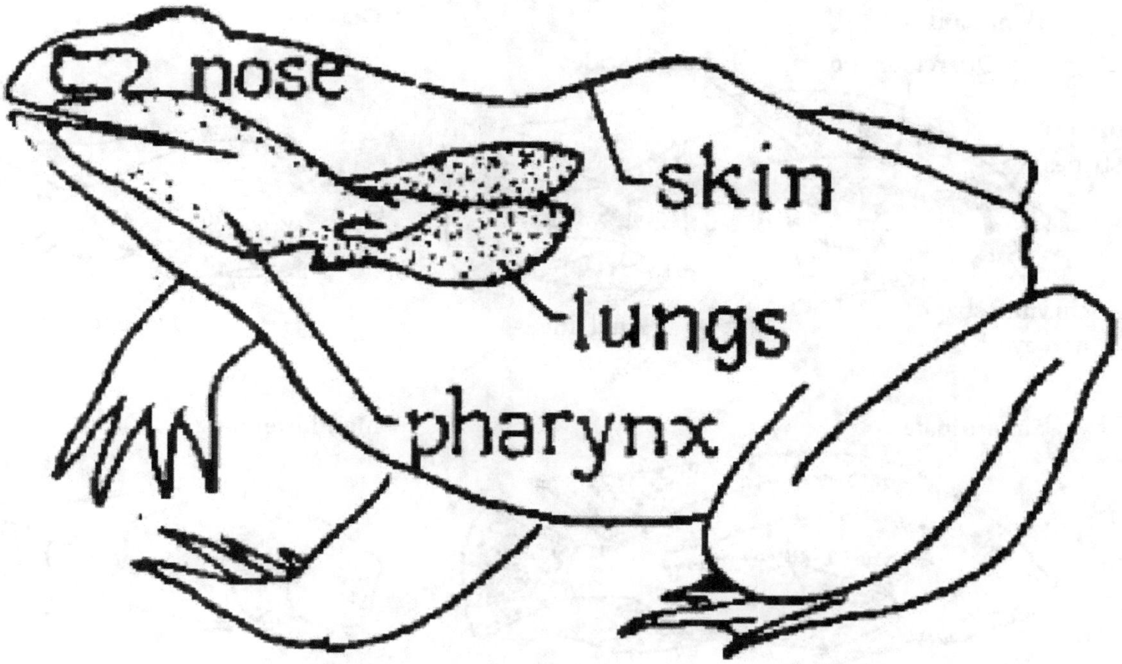


RESPIRATORY

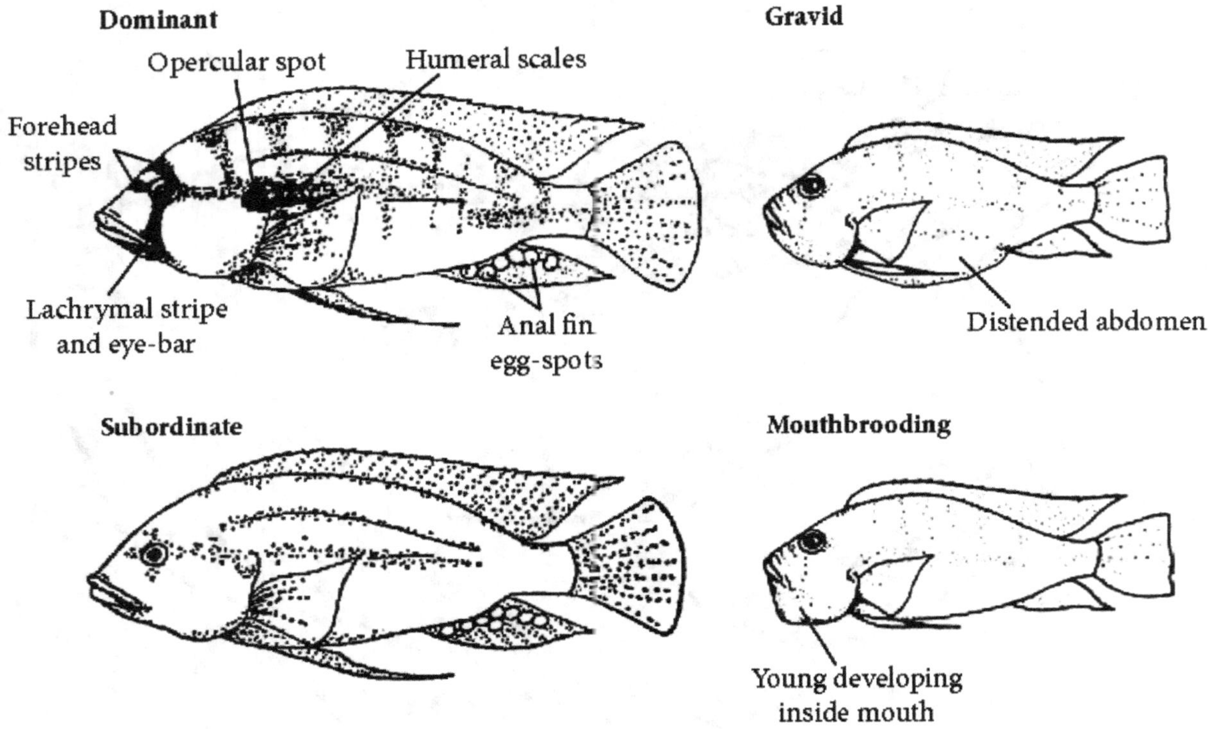
Dominant
Opercular spot
Humeral scales
Forehead stripes
Lachrymal stripe and eye-bar
Anal fin egg-spots
Gravid
Distended abdomen
Subordinate
Mouthbrooding
Young developing inside mouth

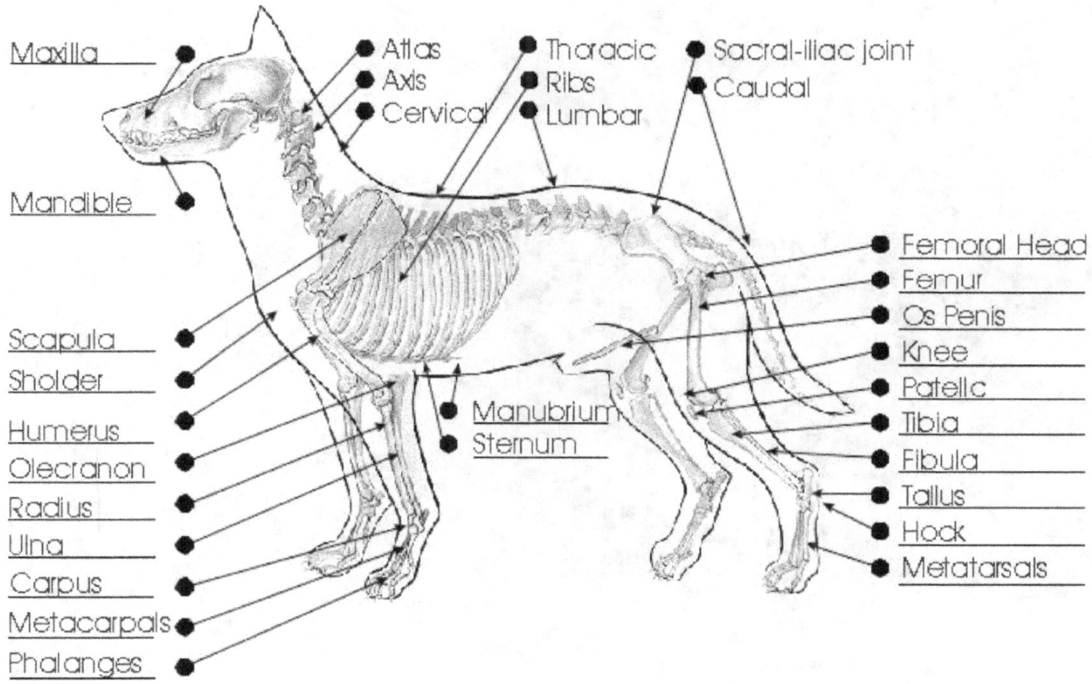

Maxilla
Atlas
Axis
Cervical
Thoracic
Ribs
Lumbar
Sacral-iliac joint
Caudal
Mandible
Femoral Head
Femur
Os Penis
Knee
Patellc
Tibia
Fibula
Tallus
Hock
Metatarsals
Scapula
Sholder
Humerus
Olecranon
Radius
Ulna
Carpus
Metacarpals
Phalanges
Manubrium
Sternum

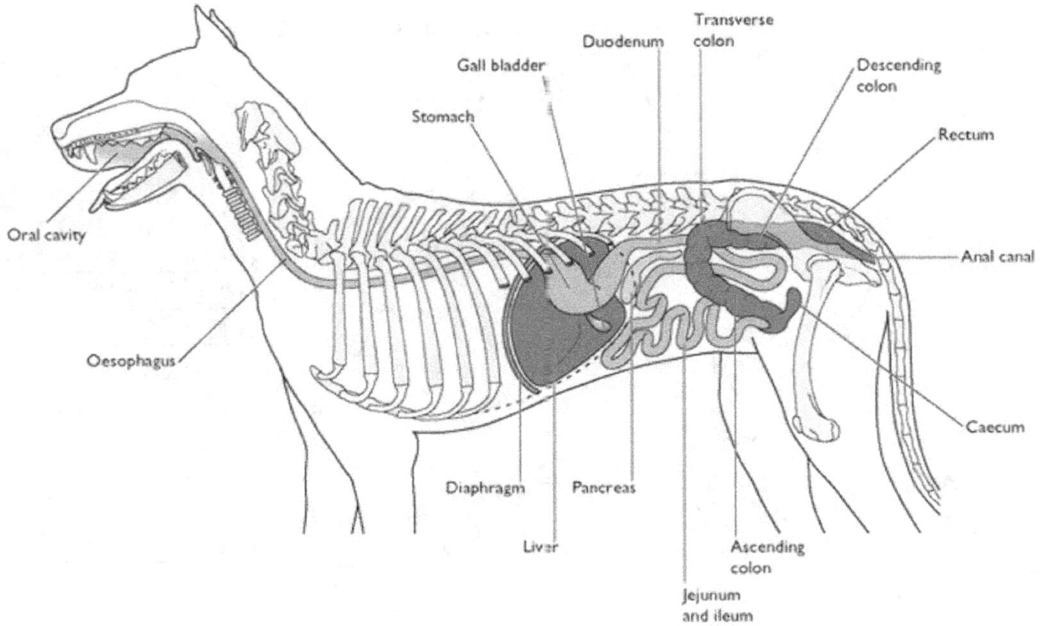
Transverse colon
Duodenum
Gall bladder
Descending colon
Stomach
Rectum
Oral cavity
Anal canal
Oesophagus
Caecum
Diaphragm
Pancreas
Liver
Ascending colon
Jejunum and ileum

# Internal Anatomy of a fish

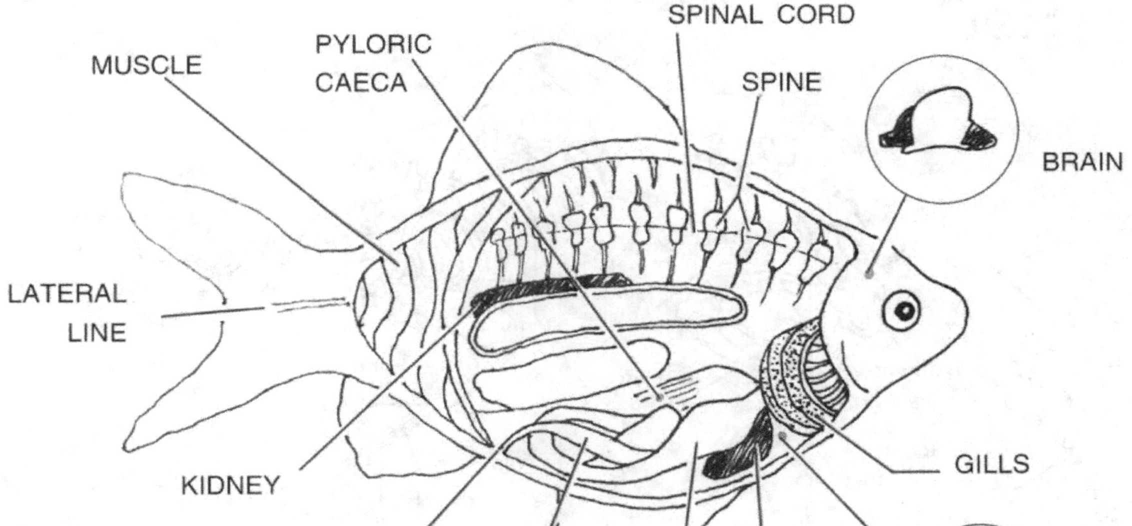

# Rat

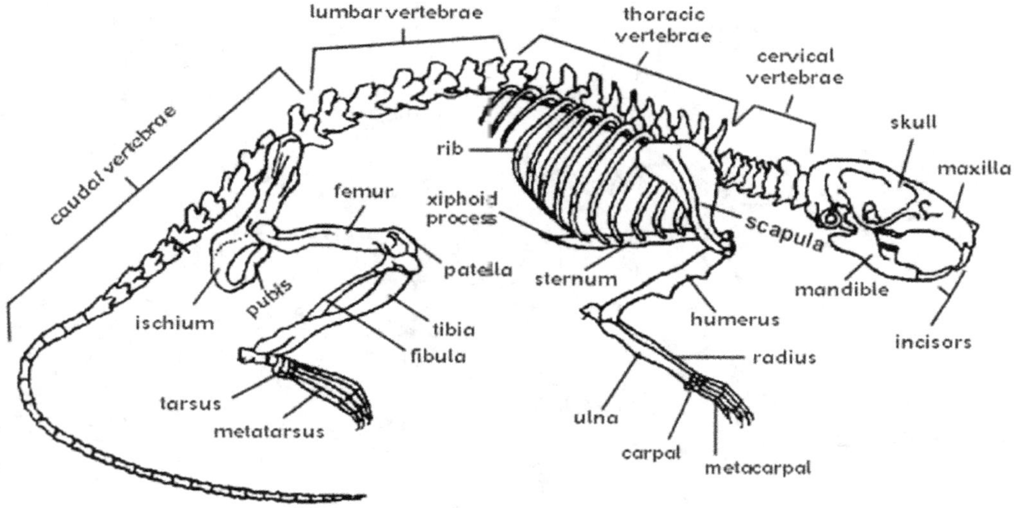

lumbar vertebrae
thoracic vertebrae
cervical vertebrae
caudal vertebrae
skull
maxilla
rib
femur
xiphoid process
scapula
patella
sternum
mandible
pubis
ischium
tibia
humerus
incisors
fibula
radius
tarsus
metatarsus
ulna
carpal
metacarpal

www.ingramcontent.com/pod-product-compliance
Lightning Source LLC
Chambersburg PA
CBHW081701220526
45466CB00009B/2848
*9798582696773*